SPOTLIGHT

KEY WEST

LAURA MARTONE

Contents

KEY WEST

KEY WEST

At the end of the Overseas Highway lies the southernmost point in the continental United States—on a quirky little island known as Key West, where biking and walking are the preferred modes of transportation. Residents here are proud to call themselves "conchs"—a remnant of the past, when Bahamian immigrants called this unique place home. To many, the Conch Republic (a term that mainly refers to Key West, though some people also apply it to the entire Florida Keys archipelago) is more than just an excuse for souvenirs; it's a symbol of the island's distinctive vibe. No wonder famous visionaries like Ernest Hemingway, Tennessee Williams, Robert Frost, and John James Audubon had such an affinity for this town.

These days Key West is home to a blend of varied folks, including vacationing families, retired couples, eccentric artists, newlyweds, adventurers, corporate escapees, and hardy natives who can withstand the humidity, isolation, and hurricane season. The island also has a sizable gay population—as evidenced by male-only resorts, gay-themed tours, and events like Fantasy Fest.

Those who have heard of Key West but never seen it for themselves often liken it to a 24-hour Mardi Gras celebration in the New Orleans French Quarter, but the Southernmost City is not so easy to characterize. In fact, it's as diverse as the rest of the Keys. While there's indeed a party vibe in some of the Old Town bars and restaurants—such as Sloppy Joe's, home to the famous Hemingway Look-Alike Contest

© LAURA MARTONE

HIGHLIGHTS

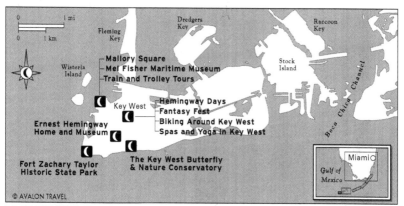

LOOK FOR ◖ TO FIND RECOMMENDED SIGHTS, ACTIVITIES, DINING, AND LODGING.

◖ **Mallory Square:** Situated in Key West's Old Town, this waterfront plaza presents several eateries, shops, monuments, and attractions, including the daily Sunset Celebration (page 13).

◖ **Mel Fisher Maritime Museum:** Besides educating visitors about marine archaeology, this impressive repository highlights many of the treasures that Mel Fisher's crew discovered in the famous *Atocha* shipwreck (page 15).

◖ **Ernest Hemingway Home and Museum:** Surrounded by lush gardens, this 19th-century mansion was once home to novelist Ernest "Papa" Hemingway, who wrote *To Have and Have Not* in the backyard studio (page 19).

◖ **The Key West Butterfly & Nature Conservatory:** Stroll amid hundreds of vibrant flowers, birds, and butterflies in a glass-enclosed habitat (page 20).

◖ **Fort Zachary Taylor Historic State Park:** Centered around an intriguing Civil War fort, Florida's southernmost state park features nature trails, a popular beach, and access to incredible snorkeling opportunities (page 22).

◖ **Train and Trolley Tours:** A 90-minute narrated tour aboard either the Conch Tour Train or the Old Town Trolley provides an overview of the city's major sights and diversions (page 26).

◖ **Hemingway Days:** In honor of Key West's most famous former resident, this annual summertime event offers an array of activities, from a marlin tournament to a Hemingway Look-Alike Contest (page 35).

◖ **Fantasy Fest:** Prior to Halloween, this zany 10-day event provides a quintessential look at Key West culture, complete with outrageous costumes, colorful parades, brazen drag queens, wet T-shirt contests, and toga parties (page 36).

◖ **Biking Around Key West:** Residents and visitors alike enjoy touring this one-of-a-kind town by bicycle. Experience its historical homes, lovely gardens, and scenic beaches (page 46).

◖ **Spas and Yoga in Key West:** Befitting this tropical paradise, several resorts and day spas provide rest and rejuvenation with a variety of massages, body treatments, and sometimes, yoga lessons (page 52).

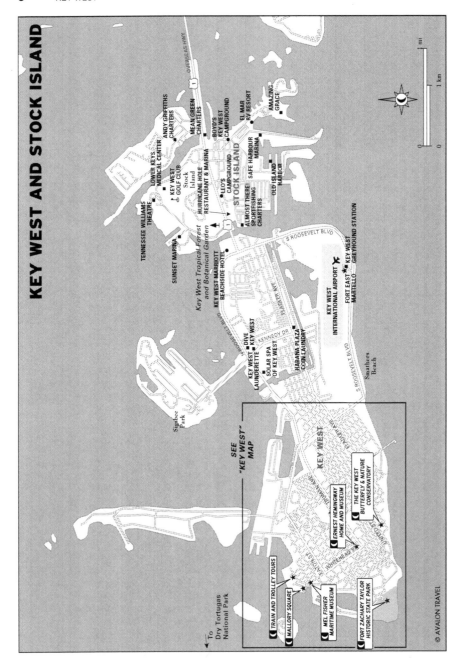

KEY WEST AND STOCK ISLAND

© AVALON TRAVEL

during the city's annual Hemingway Days—that's not all that Key West has to offer.

Old Town contains a number of Victorian inns, tropical gardens, and luxurious spas—not to mention a plethora of reliable restaurants, offering everything from fresh seafood to Caribbean cuisine to tangy key lime pie. Historical attractions abound here, too—from the Ernest Hemingway Home and Museum to the Audubon House & Tropical Gardens. Other curious diversions, like trolley tours, maritime museums, sunset celebrations at Mallory Square, and The Key West Butterfly & Nature Conservatory, can keep history buffs, relentless revelers, and nature lovers busy for days on end.

Shoppers will also find an array of enticing boutiques and emporiums. Cultural enthusiasts will be delighted by the variety of concerts and plays available. Recreationists can play golf, rent a kayak, embark on a fishing excursion, snorkel in the surrounding waters, or venture to the Dry Tortugas, and if that's not enough, Key West also hosts an assortment of festivals and events throughout the year, from the Conch Republic Independence Celebration to the Lighted Boat Parade during the winter holiday season.

Still, while Key West isn't as easy to characterize as some may believe, it is indeed a laid-back locale, where the island time seems to move at a pace all its own. As if to accentuate this easygoing persona, the tunes of Jimmy Buffett—the quintessential mascot for Key West and the Florida Keys—seem to feature prominently in every bar, restaurant, and local performer's repertoire, no matter the time of day or night.

HISTORY

During pre-Columbian times, the Calusa native people inhabited the island now known as Key West. Although Spanish explorer Juan Ponce de León was probably the first European to visit the island during his second expedition to Florida in 1521, it wasn't until Florida became a Spanish colony that a fishing and cargo-salvaging village was established here.

When initially settled by the Spanish, the island was apparently littered with bones, a fact that sparked its name: *Cayo Hueso* (Bone Island). In 1763 the British took control of Florida and relocated the community of Spaniards and Native Americans to Havana. Even after Florida returned to Spanish control in the 1780s, the island was only informally used by Cuban and Bahamian fishermen.

Key West then passed through several different hands before U.S. businessman John W. Simonton—who had been informed of the deep harbor and strategic location by his friend John Whitehead—was able to gain title to the "Gibraltar of the West." In 1822 Matthew C. Perry, who reported on piracy problems in the Caribbean, planted the U.S. flag on the island, symbolically claiming the Florida Keys for America. Although Perry tried renaming it Thompson's Island for Secretary of the Navy Smith Thompson, the name never stuck.

Soon after his purchase, Simonton subdivided the island into plots and sold some of the land to John Whitehead, John Fleming, and two men who quickly resold their share to Pardon C. Greene. Today all four of these early developers have been immortalized on the city grid in the form of street names. Other early residents of Key West include black Bahamian immigrants, known as "Conchs," who came in even larger numbers after 1830 and claimed an area west of Old Town now known as Bahama Village.

In the early 1800s, major industries in Key West included fishing, salt production, and cargo salvaging. By 1860 Key West had become the largest and richest city in Florida mainly because most of the inhabitants were salvaging high-priced cargo from shipwrecks on nearby reefs.

The latter half of the 19th century was an active period for Key West. During the American Civil War, the island remained in Union hands because of the naval base there, even though the rest of Florida joined the Confederate States of America. Fort Zachary Taylor, which was erected and fortified near Key West between 1845 and 1866, became a significant

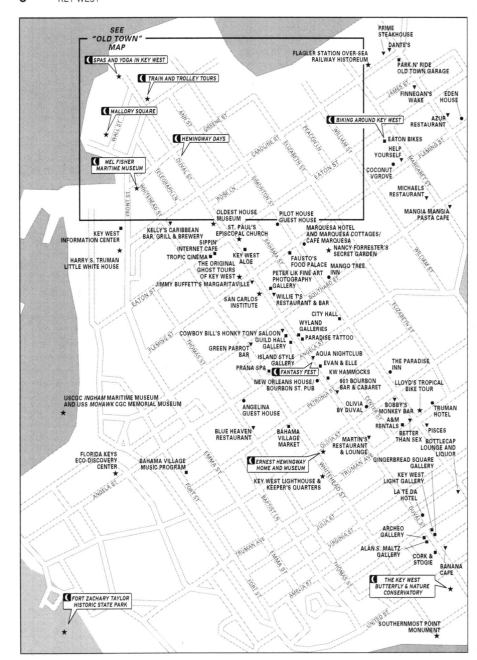

SEE "OLD TOWN" MAP

(SPAS AND YOGA IN KEY WEST

(TRAIN AND TROLLEY TOURS

(MALLORY SQUARE

(HEMINGWAY DAYS

(MEL FISHER MARITIME MUSEUM

PRIME STEAKHOUSE

DANTE'S

FLAGLER STATION OVER-SEA RAILWAY HISTOREUM

PARK N' RIDE OLD TOWN GARAGE

JAMES ST

FINNEGAN'S WAKE

EDEN HOUSE

(BIKING AROUND KEY WEST

AZUR RESTAURANT

EATON BIKES

HELP YOURSELF

COCONUT VGROVE

MICHAELS RESTAURANT

MANGIA MANGIA PASTA CAFE

WALL ST

GREENE ST

ANN ST

DUVAL ST

CAROLINE ST

ELIZABETH ST

EATON ST

PEACON LN

WILLIAM ST

FLEMING ST

MARGARET ST

ROSE LN

TELEGRAPH LN

SIMONTON ST

WILLIAM ST

FRONT ST

WHITEHEAD ST

OLDEST HOUSE MUSEUM

ST. PAUL'S EPISCOPAL CHURCH

PILOT HOUSE GUEST HOUSE

KELLY'S CARIBBEAN BAR, GRILL & BREWERY

KEY WEST INFORMATION CENTER

SIPPIN INTERNET CAFE

TROPIC CINEMA

HARRY S. TRUMAN LITTLE WHITE HOUSE

THE ORIGINAL GHOST TOURS OF KEY WEST

KEY WEST ALOE

JIMMY BUFFETT'S MARGARITAVILLE

SAN CARLOS INSTITUTE

MARQUESA HOTEL AND MARQUESA COTTAGES/ CAFÉ MARQUESA

NANCY FORRESTER'S SECRET GARDEN

FAUSTO'S FOOD PALACE

MANGO TREE INN

PETER LIK FINE ART PHOTOGRAPHY GALLERY

WILLIE T'S RESTAURANT & BAR

CITY HALL

WYLAND GALLERIES

BAHAMA ST

SOUTHARD ST

ELIZABETH ST

COWBOY BILL'S HONKY TONY SALOON

GUILD HALL GALLERY

PARADISE TATTOO

GREEN PARROT BAR

ISLAND STYLE GALLERY

AQUA NIGHTCLUB

THE PARADISE INN

FLEMING ST

THOMAS ST

PRANA SPA

(FANTASY FEST

EVAN & ELLE

KW HAMMOCKS

ANGELA ST

PETRONIA ST

NEW ORLEANS HOUSE/ BOURBON ST. PUB

801 BOURBON BAR & CABARET

LLOYD'S TROPICAL BIKE TOUR

USCGC INGHAM MARITIME MUSEUM AND USS MOHAWK CGC MEMORIAL MUSEUM

ANGELINA GUEST HOUSE

OLIVIA BY DUVAL

BOBBY'S MONKEY BAR

TRUMAN HOTEL

A&M RENTALS

PISCES

BLUE HEAVEN RESTAURANT

BAHAMA VILLAGE MARKET

MARTIN'S RESTAURANT & LOUNGE

BETTER THAN SEX

BOTTLECAP LOUNGE AND LIQUOR

CENTER ST

DUVAL ST

FLORIDA KEYS ECO-DISCOVERY CENTER

BAHAMA VILLAGE MUSIC PROGRAM

(ERNEST HEMINGWAY HOME AND MUSEUM

GINGERBREAD SQUARE GALLERY

KEY WEST LIGHT GALLERY

EMMA ST

FORT ST

ANGELA ST

KEY WEST LIGHTHOUSE & KEEPER'S QUARTERS

WHITEHEAD ST

TRUMAN AVE

LA TE DA HOTEL

BAPTIST LN

JULIA ST

VIRGINIA ST

ARCHEO GALLERY

TRUMAN AVE

EMMA ST

FORT ST

THOMAS ST

ALAN S. MALTZ GALLERY

CORK & STOGIE

BANANA CAFE

AMELIA ST

(THE KEY WEST BUTTERFLY & NATURE CONSERVATORY

(FORT ZACHARY TAYLOR HISTORIC STATE PARK

UNITED ST

SOUTHERNMOST POINT MONUMENT

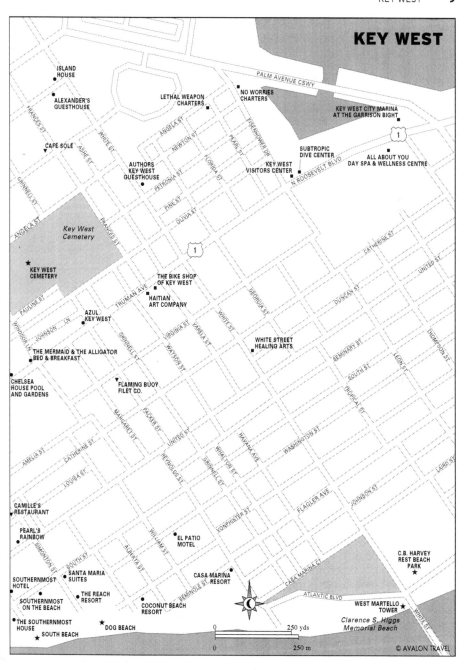

KEY WEST

ISLAND HOUSE
ALEXANDER'S GUESTHOUSE
LETHAL WEAPON CHARTERS
NO WORRIES CHARTERS
PALM AVENUE CSWY
KEY WEST CITY MARINA AT THE GARRISON BIGHT
CAFÉ SOLÉ
SUBTROPIC DIVE CENTER
ALL ABOUT YOU DAY SPA & WELLNESS CENTRE
AUTHORS KEY WEST GUESTHOUSE
KEY WEST VISITORS CENTER
N ROOSEVELT BLVD
Key West Cemetery
KEY WEST CEMETERY
THE BIKE SHOP OF KEY WEST
HAITIAN ART COMPANY
AZUL KEY WEST
WHITE STREET HEALING ARTS
THE MERMAID & THE ALLIGATOR BED & BREAKFAST
CHELSEA HOUSE POOL AND GARDENS
FLAMING BUOY FILET CO.
CAMILLE'S RESTAURANT
PEARL'S RAINBOW
EL PATIO MOTEL
C.B. HARVEY REST BEACH PARK
SANTA MARIA SUITES
CASA MARINA RESORT
SOUTHERNMOST HOTEL
THE REACH RESORT
WEST MARTELLO TOWER
SOUTHERNMOST ON THE BEACH
COCONUT BEACH RESORT
ATLANTIC BLVD
THE SOUTHERNMOST HOUSE
SOUTH BEACH
DOG BEACH
Clarence S. Higgs Memorial Beach

FRANCES ST, WHITE ST, ASHE ST, GRINNELL ST, ANGELA ST, NEWTON ST, FLORIDA ST, PETRONIA ST, PINE ST, OLIVIA ST, PEARL ST, EISENHOWER DR, CATHERINE ST, UNITED ST, PAULINE ST, TRUMAN AVE, JOHNSON LN, WINDSOR LN, GRINNELL ST, VIRGINIA ST, VARELA ST, WATSON ST, WHITE ST, GEORGIA ST, DUNCAN ST, SEMINARY ST, SOUTH ST, TROPICAL ST, THOMPSON ST, LEON ST, LAIRD ST, MARGARET ST, PACKER ST, UNITED ST, REYNOLDS ST, AMELIA ST, CATHERINE ST, LOUISA ST, HAVANA AVE, WHALTON ST, WASHINGTON ST, GRINNELL ST, FLAGLER AVE, JOHNSON ST, VONPHISTER ST, WILLIAM ST, ALBERTA ST, SIMONTON ST, SOUTH ST, SEMINOLE ST, CASA MARINA CT, WHITE ST

0   250 yds
0   250 m

© AVALON TRAVEL

outpost during the Civil War. Meanwhile, Fort Jefferson, which was constructed in the Dry Tortugas about 68 miles west of the Southernmost City, became a military prison during and after the war. The 1860s and 1870s witnessed a rise in Cuban refugees, who were responsible for pioneering Key West's cigar-making industry, which eventually upstaged the flagging cargo-salvaging and salt-producing industries in the late 1800s.

In spite of such prosperity, the city of Key West suffered a setback in the mid-1880s. During the early morning hours of April 1, 1886, a fire began in the San Carlos Hall on Duval Street. Because of high winds and inadequate firefighting equipment, the fire quickly spread through the downtown area, ultimately killing four people and destroying more than six wharves and 50 buildings, including St. Paul's Episcopal Church. Following the Great Fire of 1886, the area now known as Old Town underwent several years of restoration, resulting in such architectural gems as the red-brick Custom House on Front Street.

Despite being the largest and wealthiest city in Florida in the 1890s, Key West remained fairly isolated until it was linked to the Florida mainland via the Overseas Railroad in 1912. Although the Labor Day Hurricane of 1935 essentially destroyed the railroad and killed hundreds of residents, Key West did not remain isolated for long. By 1938 the U.S. government had completed the Overseas Highway, an extension of U.S. 1. It was also in the 1930s, and later in the 1940s, that Key West began to see an influx of celebrities, from President Harry S. Truman to writer Tennessee Williams.

Key West's most famous resident, Ernest Hemingway, spent a lot of time on the island in the late 1920s and actually lived here during the 1930s, in a lovely two-story home on Whitehead Street, which is now a tourist attraction. It was during this time, in fact, that Hemingway published several of his most famous novels, including *A Farewell to Arms* (1929), *To Have and Have Not* (1937), and *For Whom the Bell Tolls* (1940).

Despite its widespread appeal, Key West suffered a financial slump in the 1930s, which was remedied by the expansion of the naval base. By World War II, the U.S. Navy had increased its presence from 50 to 3,000 acres, which included the Naval Air Station on Boca Chica Key and the Fort Taylor Annex—later renamed the Truman Annex, after President Harry S. Truman, who used the commandant's house as his wintertime White House. It was also in the 1940s that the island literally doubled in size, with a landfill now known as New Town.

By the late 1960s, tourism was beginning to take hold in Key West. The 1970s saw an increase in cruise ships, hotels, and other tourism-related establishments. The area also saw a rise in drug trafficking during this decade, and as a result, the growing tourism industry was hit hard in the early 1980s when a U.S. Border Patrol blockade near Florida City caused an enormous traffic jam for those leaving the Florida Keys via U.S. 1. In response to this disruptive search for illegal aliens and possible drug runners, Key West and the rest of the Florida Keys briefly declared their secession from the Union in 1982, subsequently forming the Conch Republic. This incident successfully ended the Border Patrol blockade, and today is celebrated with an annual Conch Republic Independence Celebration in Key West and a similar event in Key Largo.

Nowadays tourism is still the lifeblood of Key West, whose population of about 24,650 is the largest in the Florida Keys. Nearby Stock Island and faraway Dry Tortugas National Park also benefit from tourists' dollars. Once favored among marauding pirates, the small island of Key West is today divided into two distinct halves. On the western side lies Old Town, a historical district that includes most of the city's major tourist destinations, such as Mallory Square, Fort Zachary Taylor, Duval and Whitehead Streets, and the oceanside beaches. Meanwhile, the eastern side of the island, known as New Town, comprises shopping centers, residential areas, schools, and Key West International Airport.

PLANNING YOUR TIME

With its plethora of beaches, museums, nature centers, cultural events, train and trolley tours, sunset cruises, and other outdoor activities, Key West is definitely the most active town in the Florida Keys. In fact, it's no surprise that many travelers bypass the other islands to make Key West their primary destination.

Ironically, despite its diversions, it's also the most compact region in the Florida Keys. Including adjacent Stock Island, the area stretches from Mile Marker 5 to Mile Marker 0 on the Overseas Highway, which makes this an incredibly easy town to navigate. You can walk, bike, or drive around at your own pace. In addition, taxicabs and pedicabs are available day and night—which means you can stay wherever you want, from an Old Town bed-and-breakfast to a coastal resort.

Given all that there is to see and do, you could conceivably stay a long weekend in the Southernmost City—a week if you plan an extra trip to Dry Tortugas National Park. Deciding when to visit Key West will depend on several factors, not the least of which is whether or not you hope to catch annual events like Hemingway Days, which usually takes place in mid-July, or Fantasy Fest, which typically occurs in late October. Since Key West is popular at such times, as well as during the winter months, you should be prepared for higher lodging rates, crowded restaurants and bars, and the need for reservations.

Although crime is not a huge problem in the Florida Keys, bear in mind that Key West is a city, where anything is possible. As with many other tourist havens, muggings do occur from time to time, so it's advisable to stay alert and avoid walking on desolate, poorly lit streets at night.

For more information about Key West, consult the **Monroe County Tourist Development Council** (1201 White St., Ste. 102, Key West, 305/296-1552 or 800/352-5397, www.fla-keys. com, 9am-5pm Mon.-Fri.) and the **Key West Chamber of Commerce** (510 Greene St., 1st Fl., Key West, 305/294-2587, www.keywest-chamber.org, 8am-6:30pm daily).

Sights

Of all the inhabited Florida Keys, Key West has, by far, the most museums, cultural attractions, and sightseeing tours, many of which are suitable for the entire family. Although New Town and Stock Island have a few curious locales between them, most of the tourist-friendly spots can be found in Old Town, Key West's original settlement.

OLD TOWN

Just a self-guided stroll through Old Town, part of which is a National Historic District, is a worthy attraction in itself, especially for architecture lovers. Along the way, you'll spot historical buildings like the majestic **Old City Hall** (510 Greene St.), constructed in 1891; the red-brick **Custom House** (281 Front St.), also erected in 1891 and once the workplace of Thomas Edison; and innumerable Conch-style homes, ornate Victorian mansions, and unusual eyebrow houses. While wandering the streets of Key West, you're sure to find a myriad of worthy attractions to entice you off the sidewalk—at least for a little while.

Flagler Station Over-Sea Railway Historeum

Although technically not part of Old Town, the **Historic Seaport at Key West Bight** (www.keywestseaport.com), which lies along the edge of this historical district, lures many a visitor onto the picturesque harbor walk—especially on sunny days, when it's pleasant just to amble along the waterfront, taking in the sights of majestic schooners, private yachts, and other boats in the harbor. Before completing this stroll, which stretches from Grinnell Street to Simonton, take a short detour

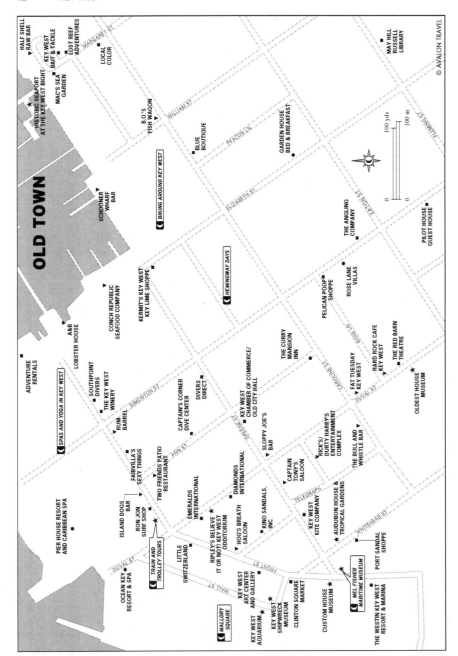

© AVALON TRAVEL

OLD TOWN

HALF SHELL RAW BAR
KEY WEST BAIT & TACKLE
LOST REEF ADVENTURES
MARGARET ST
LOCAL COLOR
MAY HILL RUSSELL LIBRARY
HISTORIC SEAPORT AT THE KEY WEST BIGHT
MAC'S SEA GARDEN
B.O.'S FISH WAGON
WILLIAM ST
GARDEN HOUSE BED & BREAKFAST
SCHOONER WHARF BAR
BLUE BOUTIQUE
PEACON LN
BIKING AROUND KEY WEST
ELIZABETH ST
THE ANGLING COMPANY
EATON ST
100 yds
100 m
SIMONTON ST
FLEMING ST
PILOT HOUSE GUEST HOUSE
HEMINGWAY DAYS
KERMIT'S KEY WEST KEY LIME SHOPPE
PELICAN POOP SHOPPE
ROSE LANE VILLAS
CONCH REPUBLIC SEAFOOD COMPANY
DUVAL ST
HARD ROCK CAFE KEY WEST
THE RED BARN THEATRE
A&B LOBSTER HOUSE
THE CURRY MANSION INN
ADVENTURE RENTALS
SPAS AND YOGA IN KEY WEST
SOUTHPOINT DIVERS
THE KEY WEST WINERY
FAT TUESDAY KEY WEST
OLDEST HOUSE MUSEUM
RUM BARREL
SIMONTON ST
KEY WEST CHAMBER OF COMMERCE/ OLD CITY HALL
CAPTAIN'S CORNER DIVE CENTER
DIVERS DIRECT
CAROLINE ST
GREENE ST
SLOPPY JOE'S BAR
RICK'S/ DURTY HARRY'S ENTERTAINMENT COMPLEX
THE BULL AND WHISTLE BAR
ANN ST
FAIRVILLA'S SEXY THINGS
TWO FRIENDS PATIO RESTAURANT
CAPTAIN TONY'S SALOON
PIER HOUSE RESORT AND CARIBBEAN SPA
ISLAND DOGS BAR
RON JON SURF SHOP
EMERALDS INTERNATIONAL
DIAMONDS INTERNATIONAL
TELEGRAPH
KEY WEST KITE COMPANY
WHITEHEAD ST
DUVAL ST
TRAIN AND TROLLEY TOURS
LITTLE SWITZERLAND
RIPLEY'S BELIEVE IT OR NOT! KEY WEST ODDITORIUM
HOG'S BREATH SALOON
KINO SANDALS, INC.
AUDUBON HOUSE & TROPICAL GARDENS
PORT SANDAL SHOPPE
OCEAN KEY RESORT & SPA
MALLORY SQUARE
KEY WEST ART CENTER AND GALLERY
WALL ST
FRONT ST
CUSTOM HOUSE MUSEUM
MEL FISHER MARITIME MUSEUM
KEY WEST AQUARIUM
KEY WEST SHIPWRECK MUSEUM
CLINTON SQUARE MARKET
THE WESTIN KEY WEST RESORT & MARINA

inland to the corner of Caroline and Margaret Streets, where you'll spot the **Flagler Station Over-Sea Railway Historeum** (901 Caroline St., 305/293-8716, www.flaglerstation.net, 9am-5pm daily, $5 adults, $2.50 children). Completed in January of 1912, the station now serves as a tribute to Henry Flagler's determination to construct a 130-mile extension of the Florida East Coast Railway all the way to Key West.

In spite of his many critics, Flagler achieved his dream, with the help of hundreds of tireless workers. Although the Labor Day Hurricane of 1935 effectively destroyed the Overseas Railroad, this historical feat is still worthy of exploration, and at the Flagler Station that's exactly what visitors can do. Here you'll encounter an assortment of intriguing artifacts, photographs, memorabilia, and eyewitness accounts. After passing through a reconstruction of the original station and a themed mercantile store, you'll step inside an actual railroad car, listen to informative storytellers, and watch various film presentations—including one about the construction of "Flagler's Folly" and another about the celebrations that took place on the day that Flagler and his wife arrived in Key West after riding the train all the way from New York.

Key West Turtle Museum

At the northern end of Margaret Street, between the Flagler Station Over-Sea Railway Historeum and the Historic Seaport at Key West Bight, lies one of the city's newest attractions: the enlightening **Key West Turtle Museum** (200 Margaret St., 305/294-0209, www.keywestturtlemuseum.org, 10am-5pm Tues.-Sat., donation suggested). Housed in a former turtle cannery and overseen by the lauded Mel Fisher Maritime Museum, this small attraction educates visitors about the long history of sea turtles in the Florida Keys. Sea turtles were a main source of sustenance for the Native American tribes that once inhabited these islands, and even the famous explorer Juan Ponce de León noted an abundance of loggerhead turtles in the surrounding waters.

In fact, he was so impressed that he named the islands Tortugas, which means "turtles" in Spanish. Unfortunately, turtle fishing nearly decimated the local sea turtle population by the early 1900s. Since the 1950s, however, conservation and rescue efforts have helped these endangered creatures by protecting their habitats, tagging them for research purposes, and promoting public awareness of their plight. Besides featuring exhibits that explore Key West's maritime history, including its negative impact on area sea turtles and the subsequent efforts by conservationists like Archie Carr to save them, the museum also presents free lectures and other family-friendly programs, such as educational summer camps.

Ripley's Believe It or Not! Key West Odditorium

Half a block southeast of Front and Duval Streets, you'll encounter the two-story 8,000-square-foot **Ripley's Believe It or Not! Key West Odditorium** (108 Duval St., 305/293-9939, www.ripleys.com/keywest, 9:30am-11pm daily, $15 adults, $9 children 5-12, free for children under 5) on Duval. While not the most unique place in town, Ripley's is still very popular among visitors, especially children. Boasting over 500 unusual exhibits in 13 themed galleries, this bizarre attraction features everything from a stuffed rare white buffalo to a portrait fashioned from butterfly wings. Also on display are some of Ernest Hemingway's former belongings, including a typewriter and a shrunken torso.

Mallory Square

Nestled alongside the Gulf of Mexico between Duval and Front Streets lies **Mallory Square** (1 Whitehead St., www.mallorysquare.com), a popular destination for residents and tourists alike. Stretching from the Ocean Key Resort to the cruise ship pier, this open-air district features several eateries and shops, such as those enclosed within the air-conditioned **Clinton Square Market.** You'll also find several attractions, including the **Key West Historic Memorial Sculpture Garden** (www.

strolling past the Key West Shipwreck Museum

keywestsculpturegarden.org), which features 36 bronze busts of the town's pioneers, and the **Key West-Florida Keys Historic Military Memorial,** which honors the city's involvement in America's major wars.

Also located here is the **Key West Shipwreck Museum** (1 Whitehead St., 305/292-8990, www.shipwreckhistoreum.com, 9:40am-5pm daily, $15 adults, $6.50 children 4-12, free for children under 4), where live performers, films, and actual artifacts let visitors experience a 19th-century wrecker's warehouse and learn about the 1856 *Isaac Allerton* shipwreck and subsequent salvage. You can also discover how Key West once became the richest city in America and even pretend to spot wrecks from the 65-foot lookout tower atop the museum, the last of 20 such towers in Key West. Just steps from the Shipwreck Museum, the **Key West Aquarium** (1 Whitehead St., 305/296-2051 or 888/544-5927, www.keywestaquarium.com, 10am-6pm daily, $15 adults, $7.50 children 4-12, free for children under 4) presents daily

shark and turtle feedings as well as hands-on touch tanks featuring starfish, queen conch, and other regional marinelife. Opened in 1934, the aquarium also offers visitors the chance to observe moray eels, barracuda, grouper, tarpon, parrotfish, sea turtles, alligators, and other sea creatures in a 50,000-gallon tank that represents a typical mangrove ecosystem in the Florida Keys.

At least once during your visit to Key West, stroll to Mallory Square in the late afternoon, when artists, musicians, acrobats, and tourists converge to pay homage to Key West's gorgeous sunsets during the daily **Sunset Celebration.** To avoid the crowds along the shore, head to The Westin Key West Resort & Marina at 245 Front Street, where you can watch the sunset while sipping cocktails on the aptly named **Sunset Deck.**

Custom House Museum

Beside the Clinton Square Market in Mallory Square stands the Custom House, a gorgeous red-brick structure erected in 1891 and once home to a post office, a courthouse, and a government center during a time when salvaging cargo from nearby shipwrecks had made Key West the wealthiest city per capita in the United States. By the 1930s, the city had gone bankrupt, and the Custom House was eventually abandoned. Following a nine-year, $9-million restoration project, the Key West Art & Historical Society opened the historical building to the public in 1999 as the Key West Museum of Art and History at the Custom House, now simply known as the **Custom House Museum** (281 Front St., 305/295-6616, www.kwahs.org, 9:30am-4:30pm daily, $7 adults, $6 seniors 62 and over and Key West residents, $5 children and students, free for children under 6) and listed in the National Register of Historic Places. Among the fascinating exhibits here you'll see Paul Collins's portraits of famous Key West residents, from Henry Flagler to Ernest Hemingway; Mario Sanchez's brightly colored wood paintings of life in Key West during the early 1900s; and various artifacts from Ernest Hemingway's adventurous life before and during his time on the island. You'll also learn about the pirates that once prowled the waters of the Florida Keys and how the U.S. Navy eventually expunged these looters and marauders from the region.

◖ Mel Fisher Maritime Museum

Not far from the hard-to-miss Custom House on Front Street stands the massive **Mel Fisher Maritime Museum** (200 Greene St., 305/294-2633, www.melfisher.org, 8:30am-5pm Mon.-Fri., 9:30am-5pm Sat.-Sun., $12.50 adults, $10.50 students, $6 children), one of the most impressive treasure collections and marine archaeology museums in the world. After passing through the gift shop just beyond the front entrance, you'll encounter an array of fascinating exhibits, the first of which explains Mel Fisher's 16-year search for the *Nuestra Señora de Atocha* and the *Santa Margarita,* two Spanish galleons that shipwrecked off the coast of the Florida Keys in 1622. Both vessels were part of a treasure fleet bound for Spain. Loaded with gold, silver, copper, tobacco, indigo, gems, and other valuables, the ships encountered a severe hurricane in early September of 1622, driving them onto the coral reefs near the Dry Tortugas and drowning many of those on board. Although Spain managed to recover some of the cargo from the *Santa Margarita,* salvagers were never able to locate the *Atocha,* which had apparently sunk in more than 50 feet of water. The shipwreck attained legendary status when Fisher's determination finally prevailed.

Subsequent museum displays feature a mere fraction of the multimillion-dollar treasures that Fisher and his crew uncovered and preserved after the 1985 discovery. Here you'll see practical items such as daggers, corroded skillets, olive jars, shackles, thimbles, even an enormous anchor. In the adjacent chamber, you'll find it hard not to be awed by the varied treasures, from gold chains and silver coins to copper chunks and tobacco leaves. Especially intriguing is the 78-carat emerald that seems to glow like plutonium.

Following an exhibit about Mel Fisher's life, you'll head upstairs for the *La Plata del Mar* exhibit, highlighting the diverse collection of silver artifacts that were carried aboard the 1622 Spanish fleet. With holy music playing in the background, you'll stroll past enormous silver bars and varied display cases filled with silver reales, goblets, mirror frames, and other intriguing items. In the adjacent rooms, you'll learn about other sunken vessels, including the 1715 Plate Fleet and the *Henrietta Marie* slave ship. After your comprehensive tour, if your yen for treasure hunting has yet to be sated, consider stopping by Mel Fisher's Treasures, a separate jewelry store in the rear of the museum. And if that's not enough, you can opt to be an investor in the ongoing salvaging efforts of the *Atocha,* which is still yielding interesting, and often incredibly valuable, finds.

Audubon House & Tropical Gardens

Directly opposite the Mel Fisher museum on Greene Street—and, oddly enough, a gigantic water tank—you'll spot the **Audubon House**

© DANIEL MARTONE

the impressive Mel Fisher Maritime Museum

& Tropical Gardens (205 Whitehead St., 305/294-2116 or 877/294-2470, www.audubonhouse.com, 9:30am-5pm daily, $12 adults, $7.50 students, $5 children 6-12, free for children under 6), one of several tranquil, historical properties in Key West. Built in 1847 by Captain John H. Geiger, a shipwreck salvager and the city's first harbormaster, this gorgeous three-story home is a quintessential example of 19th-century architecture, with a symmetrical tropical-style design that features first-floor porches, second-level balconies, white walls and columns, and dark wooden shutters. Interestingly, John James Audubon never lived here, although the celebrated naturalist presumably visited the property in 1832 during a research trip to the Florida Keys and Dry Tortugas.

Inside the lovely mansion, you'll see plenty of antiques and period furniture, though the most interesting items are the numerous original renditions and reprints of Audubon's ornithological paintings throughout the second and third floors. Among the regional species on display

the Audubon House & Tropical Gardens

are roseate spoonbills, Florida cormorants, booby gannets, brown pelicans, mangrove cuckoos, blue-headed pigeons, noddy terns, reddish egrets, and mango hummingbirds.

Following your tour of the house, feel free to meander along the brick pathways through the ecofriendly tropical gardens, shaded by palm trees and bursting with vibrant orchids and bromeliads. On your way out, take a moment to peruse the **Audubon House Gallery of Natural History,** a small art gallery near the entrance.

Harry S. Truman Little White House

Just south of Caroline and Front Streets, the Truman Annex features the **Harry S. Truman Little White House** (111 Front St., 305/294-9911, www.trumanlittlewhitehouse.com, 9am-5pm daily, $16 adults, $14 seniors, $5 children 5-12, free for children under 5 and Key West residents), another remarkable example of Key West architecture and a fascinating piece of the town's history. This breezy white structure, which was constructed in 1890 and once served as the command headquarters for the Key West Naval Station, became Truman's wintertime White House from 1946 to 1952 and later a retreat for five other U.S. presidents.

Now serving as Florida's only presidential museum and listed on the National Register of Historic Places, this restored home invites visitors to amble amid original furnishings and learn about President Truman's personal and professional life, the politics of the Cold War, the naval history of Key West, and the origin of the Department of Defense. **Guided tours** are offered every 20 minutes, between 9am and 4:30pm daily, and usually last between 45 and 55 minutes; scripts are available for the hearing-impaired. Guests can also take free self-guided tours of the adjacent **botanical gardens,** usually between 7am and 6pm daily, and the gift shop is open 9am-5pm daily. The museum offers wheelchair-accessible restrooms and allows service animals to accompany their owners onto the premises. Incidentally, parking is

the shady grounds of the Harry S. Truman Little White House

only available at Mallory Square or the Westin parking garage.

Oldest House Museum

Currently operated by the **Old Island Restoration Foundation** (OIRF, www.oirf. org), the **Oldest House Museum** (322 Duval St., 305/294-9501, 10am-4pm Mon.-Tues. and Thurs.-Sat., free) is literally the oldest house in southern Florida. Supposedly erected in 1829 by Richard Cussans, a Bahamian builder and merchant, and moved to its current location in the mid-1830s, this white one-story country-style structure was the longtime home of Captain Frances Watlington, a sea captain, shipwreck salvager, and one-time state senator. The historic home remained in the Watlington family until 1972 when it was purchased by an individual and soon afterward deeded to the Historic Key West Preservation Board.

Over the decades, the stalwart house has survived fires, hurricanes, financial hardships, even the occupation of Union troops. Though docents and staff members are available to provide historical information about the property, visitors are free to roam through the tranquil rear garden as well as the house itself, which features many family portraits, original furnishings, plus other period pieces, ship models, and documents that relate to wrecking activities.

St. Paul's Episcopal Church

No matter how you choose to explore Duval, Old Town's main drag, you'll find it hard to miss the imposing white structure on the southeastern corner of Duval and Eaton Streets. Founded in 1831, **St. Paul's Episcopal Church** (401 Duval St., 305/296-5142, www. stpaulskeywest.org, 9am-5:30pm daily, free) is the oldest church community south of St. Augustine, though the building itself is far younger. Originally constructed in 1839, the first church, made of coral rock, was leveled in an 1846 hurricane. Rebuilt in 1848, the second church, a wooden structure, was destroyed by the city's Great Fire of 1886. The third church, also made of wood, was completed in 1887 and taken by a hurricane in 1909.

The fourth incarnation of the church, the concrete structure that exists today, was designed in 1911, completed in 1919, and heavily renovated in 1993. With a striking frame, gorgeous stained-glass windows, and a traditional tin roof, St. Paul's is truly a magnificent building and the widely accepted centerpiece of downtown Key West. No wonder it's often photographed by both residents and out-of-towners. Music lovers will especially appreciate this historical sanctuary, where the organist offers free lunchtime concerts, and musical events are featured throughout the year.

San Carlos Institute

Just over a block southeast of the prominent St. Paul's Episcopal Church, you'll spot another fine example of Floridian architecture. Founded in 1871 by Cuban exiles and featuring an ornate Spanish-style facade, the **San Carlos Institute** (516 Duval St., 305/294-3887, www.institutosancarlos.org, noon-6pm Fri.-Sun., free) is one of the state's most historic landmarks. Dubbed *"La Casa Cuba"* by Cuban poet José Martí, the San Carlos was the site of Martí's 1892 attempt to unite the politically divided Cuban exile community in a bid for Cuba's independence. Today this venerable institution serves as a nonprofit multipurpose facility, featuring a museum, a library, a school, an art gallery, and a 360-seat theater that often hosts seminars and live concerts. Of particular interest to most visitors are the permanent exhibits relating to the history of Cuba and Florida's Cuban-American community, such as the photographs of poet José Martí and the portraits of Cuba's constitutional presidents.

Nancy Forrester's Secret Garden

Two blocks east of Duval Street lies a private tropical oasis that has been open to the public for years. Also known as Key West's Exotic Tropical Botanical Garden, **Nancy Forrester's Secret Garden** (1 Free School Ln., 305/294-0015, www.nancyforrester.com, 10am-5pm daily, $10 adults, $5 children 5-11) is widely celebrated for its gorgeous landscape of ferns, aroids, shade palms, edible fruits, medicinal plants, and other rare foliage—an ideal home for the macaws who live here. In the center of this enticing sanctuary stands a small cottage that has often served as an inspiring artist's studio—and can even be rented by those hoping to escape amid nature for a while.

Created by local artist and environmental educator Nancy Forrester, this lush garden is more than just a tourist attraction. It's also meant to represent the artist's wish for humanity to restore balance to the natural world. Unfortunately, this lovely spot—the last undeveloped wooded acre in the heart of Old Town—needs the public's help to remain open, so if you relish this peaceful place, consider contributing to the capital campaign on your next visit.

Key West Cemetery

On the eastern side of Old Town, you'll find the intriguing palm-lined **Key West Cemetery** (701 Passover Ln., 305/292-8177, www.keywestcity.com, 7am-7pm daily in summer, 7am-6pm daily in winter, free). Established in 1847, following a disastrous 1846 hurricane that unearthed the original cemetery, this fenced 19-acre property now contains beautiful statuary, historical gravestones, amusing epitaphs, and the remains of more than 80,000 Bahamian mariners, Cuban cigar makers, Spanish-American War veterans, soldiers and civilians, millionaires and paupers, whites and blacks, Catholics, Protestants, and Jews, and other unique individuals, illustrating Key West's incredibly diverse heritage.

Bordered by Windsor Lane and Angela, Frances, and Olivia Streets, the front entrance actually lies near the intersection of Angela and Margaret, where you can pick up a free comprehensive self-guided tour map from the office (8:30am-3:30pm Mon.-Fri.). Guided one-hour tours (9:30am Tues. and Thurs., $15 pp donation suggested) are also available through the **Historic Florida Keys Foundation** (Old City Hall, 510 Greene St., 305/292-6718, www.historicfloridakeys.org), though reservations are

Visitors can take a tour of the Key West Cemetery.

required. Whether you come alone or as part of a tour group, remember that the cemetery is still an active place of reflection, so be respectful of mourners when visiting.

Key West Lighthouse & Keeper's Quarters

Near the intersection of Truman Avenue and Whitehead Street, it's difficult to ignore the stately white lighthouse towering above the trees. Here at the **Key West Lighthouse & Keeper's Quarters** (938 Whitehead St., 305/294-0012, www.kwahs.org, 9:30am-4:30pm daily, $10 adults, $9 seniors 62 and over and Key West residents, $5 students and children, free for children under 6), you'll learn about yet another facet of the coastal town's riveting history.

Erected in 1847 on a spot 14 feet above sea level, the 66-foot-tall brick lighthouse effectively replaced the original 46-foot wooden tower on Whitehead Point, which had been built in 1825 to aid ships navigating the dangerous offshore reefs and was unfortunately destroyed in 1846 by a hurricane. In 1894 the city added a 20-foot extension to the second lighthouse, which was decommissioned by the U.S. Coast Guard in 1969. After an expensive restoration by the Key West Art & Historical Society two decades later—the same year that it was featured in a pivotal scene in *Licence to Kill* (1989)—it became the tourist attraction it is today.

Now visitors can climb the dizzying 88-step spiral staircase to a wraparound observation deck—just beneath the active 175-watt metal halide light—for an incredible 360-degree view of the verdant city. Helpful cards indicate important locales throughout Key West, including the Casa Marina resort in the distance and the grounds of the Ernest Hemingway Home down below. Also on the well-manicured grounds lies a small gift shop, plus the former keeper's quarters, constructed in 1887 to replace the original keeper's dwelling. Today the faithfully restored quarters serve as a museum, offering a look at turn-of-the-20th-century life with historical furniture, period furnishings, and old photographs. In addition, you'll find a collection of lighthouse artifacts, instruments, maps, and photographs within various exhibits that shed some light on the maritime history of the Florida Keys.

◖ Ernest Hemingway Home and Museum

Directly across the street from the Key West Lighthouse lies the **Ernest Hemingway Home and Museum** (907 Whitehead St., 305/294-1136, www.hemingwayhome.com, 9am-5pm daily, $13 adults, $6 children, free for children under 5), one of the most popular attractions in all of Key West. Built in 1851 by Asa Tift, a marine architect and salvage wrecker, the airy two-story structure features white walls and olive-green shutters, wraparound porches on both the lower and upper levels, and arched windows and doors on all sides, which invite a lot of natural light. Curiously, this island-style domicile once housed the city's most famous resident, Papa Hemingway himself, and has

© DANIEL MARTONE

the Ernest Hemingway Home and Museum, one of Key West's most famous landmarks

since become a registered National Historic Landmark. Situated amid picturesque palm trees and blooming foliage, the home invites visitors to retrace the footsteps of Ernest Hemingway, an American novelist and short-story writer known all around the world as a big-game hunter, sport fisherman, war veteran, and unabashed adventurer.

Inside the mansion, you'll see a cornucopia of memorabilia, including period furnishings, family photographs, original artwork, and war medals. The lovingly preserved home looks much as it did during the 1930s, when Hemingway and his wife Pauline lived here. Some of the docents, while happy to share stories about Hemingway, joke that they wish Hemingway's wife hadn't replaced all of the original ceiling fans with chandeliers—a decision that seems regrettable on the hottest days, when box fans can be found throughout the house.

If you're a first-time visitor to the Hemingway Home, you should definitely opt

for a 30-minute **guided tour,** available throughout the day, before exploring the grounds on your own. Beyond the house, you'll encounter a lovely pool, quiet garden nooks, a bookstore and gift shop (305/294-1575), and the Nobel Prize winner's well-preserved studio, where he spent his most productive years. It was here, after all, that he wrote and published some of his most enduring novels, nonfiction books, and short-story collections, including *A Farewell to Arms* (1929), *Death in the Afternoon* (1932), *Green Hills of Africa* (1935), and *To Have and Have Not* (1937). While here, you'll also see a plethora of six-toed felines, the descendants of Hemingway's legendary, polydactyl cats—many of whom bear the names of famous movie stars, from the calico called Audrey Hepburn to a much-photographed black-and-white cat named after classic film star Charlie Chaplin.

◖ The Key West Butterfly & Nature Conservatory

Situated near the southern end of Duval Street, **The Key West Butterfly & Nature Conservatory** (1316 Duval St., 305/296-2988 or 800/839-4647, www.keywestbutterfly.com, 9am-5pm daily, $12 adults, $9 seniors and military personnel, $8.50 children 4-12, free for children under 4) invites visitors to take a stroll through a vibrant glass-enclosed, climate-controlled habitat filled with waterfalls, trees, flowering plants, and hundreds of colorful birds and butterflies. While here, you can also learn about butterfly anatomy, physiology, life cycles, feeding, and migration in the **Learning Center,** which offers a 15-minute orientation film and an up-close view of caterpillars feeding and developing on their host plants. In addition, you can peruse Sam Trophia's kaleidoscopic creations—essentially, a variety of encased butterfly displays—inside the art gallery, **Wings of Imagination** (9am-5:30pm daily). Before leaving the nature center, be sure to browse through the wide assortment of butterfly-related items and other souvenirs in the on-site gift shop (9am-5:30pm daily). As a bonus feature, visitor parking is available in the lot behind the

HEMINGWAY'S KEY WEST

Perhaps Key West's most popular attraction, the **Ernest Hemingway Home and Museum** (907 Whitehead St., 305/294-1136, www.hemingwayhome.com) lures curious sightseers every day. Built in 1851 by marine architect Asa Tift, this two-story mansion became home to Ernest Hemingway and his second wife, Pauline Pfeiffer, in 1931. Today visitors can see descendants of his six-toed felines, plenty of original artwork and family photographs, and the separate writing studio where the Nobel Prize-winning novelist penned several famous short stories and books, including To Have and Have Not (1937), the story of a fishing boat captain who runs contraband between Cuba and Florida.

Naturally, this isn't the sole remnant of Hemingway's time in Key West. Not only does every train, trolley, and walking tour mention his name, but you'll also find some of his former belongings in places like **Ripley's Believe It or Not! Key West Odditorium** (108 Duval St.) and the **Custom House Museum** (281 Front St.). In addition, several hotels and watering holes claim ties to Papa Hemingway. The private Mediterranean Revival-style home known as **Casa Antigua** (314 Simonton St.), for instance, was once a residential hotel above a Ford dealership, and it was here that Hemingway and Pauline stayed during their first visit to Key West. He even finished the initial draft of A Farewell to Arms (1929) while awaiting the delivery of his new Model A. Supposedly, Hemingway also stayed at **The Southernmost House** (1400 Duval St.), and he frequented **Captain Tony's Saloon** (428 Greene St.) when it was the original location of Sloppy Joe's. Today you'll even catch a glimpse of Hemingway's former bar stool. Meanwhile, the most recent incarnation of **Sloppy Joe's Bar** (201 Duval St.) features the famous Hemingway Look-Alike Contest, part of the annual **Hemingway Days** celebration in July.

Hemingway first came to Key West in 1928. For the next few years, he and Pauline spent winters in the Florida Keys and summers in Europe and Wyoming. Then in 1931, they acquired the house at 907 Whitehead Street. During this prolific period, his schedule consisted of writing every morning and relaxing every afternoon and evening with his friends. One particularly close pal was Joe Russell, an irascible fisherman and owner of Sloppy Joe's, a speakeasy. Russell introduced Hemingway to deep-sea fishing; Hemingway repaid the favor by immortalizing his friend as Harry Morgan, captain of the Queen Conch in To Have and Have Not. The backyard drinking fountain that Hemingway built for his cats is actually a refurbished urinal from Sloppy Joe's, which was also where Hemingway met reporter Martha Gellhorn in 1936, who would later become his third wife.

Originally, Hemingway's home was surrounded by a chain-link fence, but in 1935 he erected the perimeter wall that exists today, in the hope of providing his family privacy from gawking tourist hordes. Between 1937 and 1938, while Hemingway was serving as a war correspondent for the Spanish Civil War, Pauline supervised the construction of the first residential swimming pool in Key West. When he returned, he was shocked by the final price tag of $20,000, at which point he removed a penny from his pocket and told her that she might as well take his last cent. Today you can see this penny embedded beside the pool.

Hemingway stayed in Key West for well over a decade before divorcing Pauline in 1940, marrying Martha, and heading to Cuba. Pauline, meanwhile, stayed in the Key West home until her death in 1951. Upon Hemingway's death in 1961, the Key West home was sold to local businesswoman Bernice Dickson, who turned it into a museum in 1964. The home, which was designated a National Historic Landmark in 1968, remains the property of Dickson's family, though Hemingway's spirit is alive and well.

The Key West Butterfly & Nature Conservatory

conservatory, but the gate closes at 6pm every day. Although the conservatory is technically open until 5pm each day, the last tickets are sold at 4:30pm.

SOUTHERN SHORE

Along the Atlantic Ocean side of Key West lie several interesting attractions, from military monuments to marine exhibits to fantastic beaches.

Fort Zachary Taylor Historic State Park

Accessible via the western end of Southard Street, **Fort Zachary Taylor Historic State Park** (601 Howard England Way, 305/292-6713 or 305/295-0037, www.floridastateparks.org/forttaylor or www.fortzacharytaylor.com, 8am-sunset daily, $7 vehicles with 2-8 passengers plus $0.50 pp, $4.50 motorcycles and single-occupant vehicles, $2.50 pedestrians, bikers, and extra passengers) is, in fact, the southernmost state park in Florida—and, for

that matter, the continental United States. It's also a well-favored destination among history buffs and recreationists alike.

Situated at the convergence of the Gulf of Mexico and the Atlantic Ocean, where the clear, deep waters nurture living coral, yellowtail snapper, tropical fish, lobster, and other marine creatures, the 54-acre park is especially popular with swimmers, snorkelers, scuba divers, sunbathers, and picnickers, not to mention wedding parties. Enhanced by imported sand, the beach here is generally considered the finest in Key West—and an ideal place to watch an incredible Florida Keys sunset. Bikers, hikers, anglers, and bird-watchers also enjoy spending time in this beautiful place. Beyond biking paths and wooded nature trails, other amenities include picnic tables, barbecue grills, public restrooms, outdoor showers, ample parking, as well as beach equipment and water-sports rentals, such as chairs, rafts, and snorkeling gear. In addition, the Cayo Hueso Café offers refreshments from 10am to 5pm daily.

But, of course, it's the 19th-century fort that lures many visitors to this historical state park. Completed in 1866, it was critical during the American Civil War and Spanish-American War and designated a National Historic Landmark in 1973. Although you're free to wander through the fort on your own, you can also opt for one of the narrated 30-minute tours, which are available daily at noon. You'll especially enjoy visiting Fort Zachary Taylor during annual events, such as Civil War Days in February and the Conch Republic Independence Celebration in April, so be sure to plan your visit accordingly.

Florida Keys Eco-Discovery Center

From Southard Street, you can head west toward the Truman Waterfront, where you'll spy the **Florida Keys Eco-Discovery Center** (35 E. Quay Rd., 305/809-4750, www.floridakeys.noaa.gov, 9am-4pm Tues.-Sat., free). The 6,000-square-foot nature center features an array of interactive exhibits, dioramas, and displays about the Keys' varied ecosystems,

Water surrounds Fort Zachary Taylor.

including upland pinelands, hardwood hammocks, beach dunes, mangrove shores, seagrass flats, and coral reefs. Visitors can take a virtual 1,600-foot dive to the deep shelf; learn why a fort was built in the isolated Dry Tortugas; view a 2,500-gallon reef tank, filled with living coral and tropical fish; and walk through a mock-up of Aquarius, the world's only underwater ocean laboratory. Free parking is available on-site, and all net proceeds from the gift shop directly fund educational programs at the Eco-Discovery Center.

USCGC Ingham Maritime Museum
Military-history enthusiasts might enjoy a quick detour to Memorial Park, which holds the **USCGC Ingham Maritime Museum** (Truman Waterfront, Old U.S. Navy Pier, 305/292-5072, www.uscgcingham.org, 10am-4pm daily, $10 adults, $6 children 12-18, free for children under 12 and military personnel), a historical 327-foot U.S. Coast Guard cutter that was built in 1935 and served the nation from 1936 to 1988. Visitors can take

a self-guided tour of the ship, which includes authentic artifacts, historical photographs, and interpretive signs outlining the ship's history. While on board, you'll be able to see where the men ate, slept, and played, and for an added fee ($20 pp), you can take a guided tour that includes additional chambers like the boiler room and engine room.

Nearby is the floating **USS Mohawk CGC Memorial Museum** (305/292-5072, www.uscgcmohawk.org, 10am-4pm daily, $6 adults, $3 children 10-18, free for children under 10 and military personnel), a former World War II combat ship that was involved in 14 attacks against Nazi submarines. Built in 1934, this historical U.S. Coast Guard cutter now serves as a memorial to the battles fought in the Atlantic Ocean. Though retired from active duty, the 165-foot-long *Mohawk* is still fully operational, a rarity among decommissioned World War II vessels. Visitors here can watch a brief orientation film, then take a self-guided tour of various chambers, featuring artifacts, photographs, and interpretive signs. The main

one of several intriguing exhibits at the Florida Keys Eco-Discovery Center

deck, which is accessible to wheelchairs, also welcomes strollers, making this an ideal stop for families on vacation. Combination adult tickets ($15 pp) are available for those wanting to visit both ships. In addition, parking is available on-site, though you can also walk to the floating maritime museums from Southard Street.

Southernmost Point Monument

Located at the corner of South and Whitehead Streets, right beside the Atlantic Ocean, stands an enormous replica of a marine buoy that marks the southernmost point in the continental United States. Once designated by a mere sign, the spot gained the now-famous monument in 1983, when city officials grew tired of replacing the oft-stolen sign. Colorfully painted in red, yellow, black, and white, the marker simply reads "Southernmost Point Continental U.S.A." Also emblazoned on the monument are the phrases "The Conch Republic," "90 Miles to Cuba," and "Key West, FL, Home of the Sunset." Today it's one of the most photographed attractions in all of Key West, as evidenced by the frequently long line of visitors, waiting for their chance to pose in front of the colorful buoy—smaller versions of which are often seen throughout the city, on everything from shot glasses to key chains to playing cards.

Beaches

Several public beaches, ranging in size and appeal, stretch along the southern shore of Key West. The good news is that all of them are free and open daily, but the bad news is that they're often crowded, especially on a gorgeous weekend during the peak winter season. Just remember that swimming is at your own risk, given the absence of lifeguards. In addition, just because Key West has several clothing-optional resorts doesn't mean that such a flexible policy extends to the beaches down here; topless and nude sunbathing is actually illegal. Alcohol, drugs, campfires, glass containers, and overnight camping are also not allowed on the public beaches of Key West.

At the terminus of Duval Street, you'll first

encounter **South Beach** (7am-11pm daily, free), a cute patch of sand that's a far cry from the similarly named one in Miami. While it offers shallow waters, a pleasant pier, and an incredible view of the ocean, it's much smaller—and calmer—than its counterpart a few hours north. Nevertheless, it's a favorite among locals, despite the lack of restrooms and facilities. East of Simonton, the somewhat rocky **Dog Beach** (7am-11pm daily, free) is obviously popular among pet owners, though it has no restrooms or other facilities. Farther east, alongside Atlantic Boulevard between Reynolds and White Streets, lies another popular Key West beach, the wide sandy **Clarence S. Higgs Memorial Beach** (6am-11pm daily, free), where in addition to swimming and sunbathing, sun worshipers can rent water-sports equipment or stroll amid pelicans and seagulls on the adjacent swimming pier. Other on-site amenities include covered picnic tables, public restrooms, a playground, and chair rentals.

Even farther east, near Atlantic Boulevard and White Street, the wheelchair-accessible **C. B. Harvey Rest Beach** (7am-11pm daily, free) offers sandy dunes, picnic tables, public restrooms, a fishing pier, a yoga deck, and a biking path. Of course, on warm, sunny days, crowds flock to lengthy, artificially made **Smathers Beach** (7am-11pm daily, free) alongside Roosevelt Boulevard, a popular spot for spring breakers and an ideal place to watch the sunrise, have a picnic, or play a volleyball game. Water-sports and chair rentals, biking paths, concession stands, public restrooms, a boat ramp, and ample parking are also available here. **Sunset Watersports Key West** (305/296-2554, www.sunsetwatersportskey-west.com, 9am-6pm daily, $49 pp) even offers parasailing excursions from here.

West Martello Tower

On Higgs Beach, where White Street meets the Atlantic Ocean, stands the **West Martello Tower**, a Civil War-era fort that, as with the Fort East Martello Museum, was inspired by

© DANIEL MARTONE

the swimming pier that extends from Clarence S. Higgs Memorial Beach

the round, stalwart fortress at Mortella Point in Corsica, an island in the Mediterranean Sea. Constructed during the 1860s by the U.S. Army Corps of Engineers, the West Martello Tower was never fully completed, and in the late 1940s, it was nearly leveled for aesthetic reasons. Luckily, demolition plans were thwarted, and it has since been listed on the National Register of Historic Places.

Home to the **Key West Garden Club** (1100 Atlantic Blvd., 305/294-3210, www.keywestgardenclub.com, 9:30am-5pm daily, free) since 1955, this historical locale entices visitors to stroll along brick pathways, amid graceful arches and lush colorful foliage, which features a rare collection of blooming orchids, bromeliads, and other native and exotic flora. Here you can simply sit beside a water lily pond or butterfly garden, enjoy balmy breezes from an oceanfront gazebo, and temporarily trade the hustle and bustle of places like Mallory Square and Duval Street for the tranquil seclusion of a fort by the sea. The facility is closed during the first two weeks of January.

NEW TOWN AND STOCK ISLAND

Although the bulk of Key West's attractions are spread throughout Old Town, you'll find a few worthy stops in New Town, the eastern half of the island, as well as on adjacent Stock Island.

Fort East Martello

South of Key West International Airport stands **Fort East Martello** (3501 S. Roosevelt Blvd., 305/296-3913, www.kwahs.org, 9:30am-4:30pm daily, $7 adults, $5 seniors 62 and over, children, students, and Key West residents, free for children under 6). Modeled after the nearly impenetrable Martello watchtowers of Corsica and other places around the world, Fort East Martello, which was constructed during the Civil War, never actually witnessed hostile action. A testament to military engineering, the fort now serves as the country's best-preserved example of the Martello style of military architecture. Today its citadel, courtyard, and casemates house a vast array of regional artifacts,

historical records, and military memorabilia, in addition to the state's largest collection of drawings and painted wood carvings by artist Mario Sanchez, mainly known for his vivid depictions of life in Key West during the early 1900s. While here, visitors can also tour an 80-year-old playhouse and enjoy panoramic views from atop the central tower.

The Key West Tropical Forest & Botanical Garden

Besides the plethora of flowers, trees, and creatures throughout Key West, nature lovers will find several intriguing attractions—not the least of which is **The Key West Tropical Forest & Botanical Garden** (5210 College Rd., Stock Island, 305/296-1504, www.keywestbotanicalgarden.org, 10am-4pm daily, $7 adults, $5 seniors and military personnel, free for children under 12), the only frost-free botanical garden in the continental United States. Host to various events throughout the year, including Gardenfest Key West, Hot Havana Nights, and the Doo Wop Party, this tropical oasis nurtures rare flora and fauna and serves as a migratory stop for a variety of neotropical birds. After viewing a short orientation film, visitors are welcome to take a self-guided tour of the grounds, featuring a one-acre butterfly habitat, a lush canopy of tropical palms, and two of the last remaining freshwater ponds in the Florida Keys. Parking is free here, and the garden boardwalk is wheelchair-accessible.

ISLAND TOURS

If you're a first-time visitor to Key West, you might benefit from one of the many available sightseeing tours, which will help orient you to the island and its surrounding waters. So before you explore the area on your own, consider choosing from an array of trolley excursions, guided strolls, sunset cruises, or other informative tours.

◖ Train and Trolley Tours

Before exploring the town on foot, consider taking a 90-minute narrated excursion on the **Conch Tour Train** (305/294-5161 or

GAY KEY WEST TROLLEY TOUR

Featuring a plethora of gay bars, drag shows, gay and lesbian accommodations, and outrageous events like the annual Fantasy Fest, Key West is indeed a gay-friendly destination. That said, it seems appropriate that the Southernmost City would also be home to the Gay Key West Trolley Tour ($25 pp), a fun, interesting, and often hilarious private charter tour that runs every Saturday at 4pm. This 75-minute narrated excursion, which typically leaves from the corner of Angela and Duval Streets, invites visitors to hop aboard a rainbow-hued trolley and learn about the curious history of this spirited town, from its unique architecture to its wreck-salvaging heritage to its famous residents like Ernest Hemingway.

Of course, given the tour's particular theme, you'll also see gay and lesbian hot spots, hear about previous homosexual visitors such as playwright Tennessee Williams and poet Elizabeth Bishop, and hopefully come to understand the impact that gays and lesbians have had on the culture, politics, and economy of the Florida Keys. For tour tickets as well as information about other gay-friendly establishments, events, and activities, consult the **Key West Business Guild Office & Gay Key West Visitor Center** (513 Truman Ave., 305/294-4603 or 800/535-7797, www.gaykeywestfl.com), incidentally one of the oldest LGBT Chamber of Commerce organizations in the United States.

888/916-8687, www.conchtourtrain.com, 9am-4:30pm daily, $30 adults, $27 seniors and military personnel, free for children under 13 and Key West residents), which offers a look at most of Key West's major attractions, including Mallory Square, the Custom House, and the Ernest Hemingway Home. Since 1958, friendly train "engineers" have been guiding visitors around the Southernmost City and along the way sharing snippets of the town's history—real and legendary.

Train tours depart every 30 minutes from the Front Street depot (501 Front St.), where you can purchase tickets beforehand. You can also pick up tickets at three other locations: Mallory Square (303 Front St.), Flagler Station (901 Caroline St.), and 3840 North Roosevelt Boulevard. To save some money, purchase your tickets online or consider buying packages that also include admission to attractions like the Key West Aquarium and the Harry S. Truman Little White House.

As an alternative, you can take the 90-minute **Old Town Trolley Tour** (305/296-6688 or 888/910-8687, www.trolleytours.com, 9am-4:30pm daily, $30 adults, $27 seniors and military personnel, free for children under 13), which offers a comprehensive tour of Old

Town, fully narrated by expert conductors. Along the route, you'll get an earful of curious anecdotes and well-researched historical tidbits. At no extra charge, you're welcome to get on and off the trolley at a dozen convenient stops, including the Bahama Village Market. The ubiquitous orange-and-green trolleys pick up and drop off passengers every 30 minutes at each location. Tickets can be purchased at four different stops: Mallory Square (No. 1) near Wall and Whitehead Streets, Simonton Row (No. 3) at Greene and Simonton Streets, Truval Village (No. 11) at Truman Avenue and Duval Street, and Angela Street (No. 12) between Duval and Whitehead Streets. As with the Conch Tour Train, you can save a little money by purchasing tickets online. Ticket packages and wheelchair-accessible vehicles are also available.

Biking and Walking Tours

For a more active exploration of the city, consider taking **Lloyd's Tropical Bike Tour** (601 Truman Ave., 305/294-1882 or 305/304-4700, www.lloydstropicalbiketour.com, $39 pp with bicycle rental), a leisurely, ecofriendly ride along Key West's quiet streets and secret lanes, amid tropical gardens, historical architecture, and the exotic scents of jasmine and gardenias. Led by a longtime resident of Key West, these one-of-a-kind two-hour tours even enable you to taste a variety of local fruit, such as mangoes, coconuts, and key limes. The bicycles included on this tour are single-speed beach cruisers, equipped with foot brakes, fat tires, wide seats, and convenient baskets—ideal features for novice riders. Children are welcome if accompanied by at least one adult, and reservations are a must. Be sure to wear comfortable clothes and shoes, and bring your own hat, sunglasses, and sunscreen.

If you'd prefer a two-hour walking tour instead, you're in luck. There are several such tours available in Key West, including the **Historic Key West Walking Tour** (305/292-8990, www.trustedtours.com, 10am, 2pm, and 4pm daily Nov.-Apr., 9:30am daily May-Oct., $18 adults, $9 children 4-12, free for children under 4), an entertaining tour of Old Town's lush foliage, unique architecture, varied districts, and diverse culture. Along the tour, guides will share stories about the town's early inhabitants, famous and notorious Key West personalities, historic incidents like the Great Fire of 1886, and the island's varied phases, from its wrecking and cigar-making days to its involvement in both World Wars. Tours depart from the Key West Shipwreck Museum in Mallory Square. Given the limited group size, reservations are recommended. In addition, visitors should wear comfortable shoes, bring bottled water, and check in 15 minutes before departure time.

As an alternative, you can opt for **Trails and Tales of Key West** (305/292-2040, www.trailsandtalesofkeywest.net, 4pm daily, $20 pp, free for children under 12), a zany two-hour walking tour that begins at Captain Tony's Saloon, winds through Old Town and alongside the Historic Seaport, and ends at Jimmy Buffett's Margaritaville. En route, you'll learn about the history of the Conch Republic, including stories about the city's celebrated former residents, from novelist Ernest Hemingway to treasure hunter Mel Fisher to the ever-popular singer-songwriter Jimmy Buffett. Given the limited

group size, reservations are required, and comfortable shoes are highly recommended.

If your interests run toward the paranormal, you may appreciate a nighttime stroll with **The Original Ghost Tours of Key West** (423 Fleming St., 305/294-9255, www.hauntedtours.com, 8pm and 9pm nightly, $15 adults, $10 children). Founded in 1996 by David L. Sloan, author of *Ghosts of Key West,* and featured in numerous television programs, this lantern-led walking tour departs nightly from the Crowne Plaza Key West at 430 Duval Street. With a colorful history that includes pirates, smugglers, and wreckers, the town formerly known as Bone Island has its share of curious hauntings, in places as varied as the Banyan Resort, St. Paul's Episcopal Church, the Fort East Martello Museum, and Captain Tony's Saloon—all of which this 90-minute wheelchair-accessible tour encompasses. Reservations are recommended. Many of the same sites are visited through **The Ghosts & Legends of Key West** (305/294-1713, www.keywestghosts.com, 7pm and 9pm nightly, $18 adults, $10 children), a 90-minute narrated tour along the shadowy streets and lanes of Old Town. Along this route, you'll learn about Key West's most intriguing legends and bizarre ghost stories, including tales of island pirate lore, haunted Victorian mansions, and voodoo rituals. The tour departs from the Porter House Mansion at Duval and Caroline Streets, and as with the other walking tours, reservations are recommended.

Boat Tours

Since many of Key West's most memorable attractions actually lie in the waters surrounding the island, you should make some time for one of the many sightseeing cruises available, such as a two-hour glass-bottom boat tour with **Fury Water Adventures** (305/296-6293 or 877/994-8898, www.furycat.com, noon-2pm and 2pm-4pm daily, $40 adults, $20 children 6-12, free for children under 6). From aboard *The Pride of Key West,* a modern smooth-sailing catamaran, you'll be able to gaze at dolphins, sharks, and other marine creatures from the comfort of an upper sun deck or, for an even better experience, observe the colorful coral and tropical fish *below* the boat from the enclosed, air-conditioned viewing area. Other onboard amenities include restrooms and a snack bar. The catamaran leaves twice daily from the marina at 2 Duval Street, between the Ocean Key Resort and the Pier House Resort.

For a more romantic adventure, spend the evening on a sunset cruise. Among those available, Fury offers the two-hour Commotion on the Ocean (305/294-8899 or 877/994-8898, 5:30pm-7:30pm daily late Jan.-mid-Mar., 6:30pm-8:30pm daily mid-Mar.-mid-Sept., 6pm-8pm daily mid-Sept.-Oct., 5pm-7pm daily Nov.-late Jan., $50 adults, $25 children 6-12, free for children under 6), which, in conjunction with the Hog's Breath Saloon, features appetizers, beer, margaritas, and live music amid a famous Key West sunset. As a bonus, Fury donates a percentage of all sales to coral reef conservation.

As an alternative, **Sunset Watersports Key West** (201 William St., 305/296-2554, www.sunsetwatersports.info, times vary seasonally, $59 pp) offers a daily two-hour sunset yacht excursion that features a tropical buffet and a variety of libations, from soft drinks to champagne. Couples will especially enjoy watching the sunset together and dancing on the lighted dance floor. Reservations are required for the sunset dinner cruise as well as for the basic two-hour sunset cruise ($35 pp without dinner).

Other area possibilities include **Sebago Watersports** (201 William St., 305/292-4768 or 800/507-9955, www.keywestsebago.com, 5pm-7pm daily late Oct.-late Feb., 5:30pm-7:30pm daily late Feb.-early Mar., 6:30pm-8:30pm daily early Mar.-mid-Sept., 5:30pm-7:30pm daily mid-Sept.-late Oct., $39 pp), which includes free champagne, margaritas, and other libations on its catamaran champagne sunset sail.

A truly memorable experience awaits you aboard a classic schooner, such as the 80-foot, square-rigged, Caribbean-style **Schooner Jolly II Rover** (800/979-3370, www.schoonerjollyrover.com), which offers two-hour sunset sails (times vary seasonally, $39 pp) and 1.5-hour stargazer sails (8:30pm, $45 pp) every day, all of which depart from the Historic Seaport at Key West Bight. You can also opt for sunset and stargazer sails aboard the **Schooner Western Union** (305/292-1766, www.schoonerwesternunion.com, times vary daily, $59 adults, $29 children 5-12, free for children under 5), a historical tall ship and floating maritime museum that also docks at the Historic Seaport. Unlike the *Jolly II Rover,* which invites you to bring your own food and beverages, the *Western Union,* which is listed on the National Register of Historic Places, provides complimentary libations, conch chowder, and live, island-style music with each sail.

Among other excursions, **Sebago Watersports** (201 William St., 305/292-4768 or 800/507-9955, www.keywestsebago.com) features two-hour day sails (2pm-4pm daily, $45 pp) and champagne sunset sails (5pm-7pm daily in winter, 6:30pm-8:30pm daily in summer, $49 pp) aboard the **Schooner**

© DANIEL MARTONE

the Schooner *Western Union,* docked in the Historic Seaport at Key West Bight

Appledore V. Other possible adventures include a daily two-hour Wind and Wine Sunset Sail through **Danger Charters** (305/304-7999, www.dangercharters.com, times vary seasonally, $70 adults, $45 children 4-12, free for children under 4), based out of The Westin Hotel Marina at Whitehead and Greene Streets, as well as classic 1.5-hour day sails (1:30pm daily, $45 pp) and two-hour champagne sunset sails (times vary seasonally, $75 pp) aboard the **Schooner *America 2.0*** (305/293-7245, www.sail-keywest.com), which is based out of the Historic Seaport at Key West Bight and limited to a November-April sailing season. Most of the sails offered in Key West feature online discounts and recommend advance purchases.

Air Tours

If you'd like to experience an aerial tour of Key West and its surrounding waters, consider taking a biplane ride through **Key West Biplanes** (3469 S. Roosevelt Blvd., 305/851-8359 or 305/294-8687, www.keywestbiplanes.com, 10am-sunset daily). Flying out of the Key West International Airport, each narrated tour invites two passengers (besides the pilot) to view coral reefs, shipwrecks, lighthouses, uninhabited islands, and various marine creatures from aboard an original open-air 1942 World War II Waco biplane, at a smooth, 500-foot cruising altitude. You can choose from three different flights: an 18-minute Island Biplane Ride ($160 per ride) that offers a look at nearby shipwrecks; a 35-minute Island and Reef Tour ($285 per ride) that surveys coral reefs as well as Key West attractions; and a romantic 35-minute Sunset Flight ($335 per ride), which is essentially the Island and Reef Tour at sunset. Tour times are flexible, and each quoted price includes two passengers. Cloth helmets, headsets, and goggles are provided with all flights—all of which are wheelchair-accessible—and as a bonus, an on-board camera system can record your flight for posterity. Although walk-ins are welcome, reservations will ensure availability.

Entertainment and Events

NIGHTLIFE

If you like to prowl the streets at night, seeking out spirited bars, live music, and the like, then you've come to the right town. With a slew of late-night watering holes, hotel lounges, piano bars, and other entertainment options at your fingertips, Key West promises the most fun you'll have outside of the New Orleans French Quarter. Of course, Duval Street offers the largest concentration of nightlife selections—hence the term "Duval crawl," a popular activity whereby locals and visitors alike endeavor to stop by every bar along the street, from the Atlantic Ocean to the Gulf of Mexico.

Beyond the late-night chain establishments on Duval, such as the **Hard Rock Cafe Key West** (313 Duval St., 305/293-0230, www.hardrock.com, 11am-close daily) and **Jimmy Buffett's Margaritaville Key West** (500 Duval St., 305/292-1435, www.margaritavillekeywest. com, 11am-midnight daily), you'll spot unique, laid-back establishments like **Willie T's Restaurant & Bar** (525 Duval St., 305/294-7674, www.williets.com, 11am-2am daily), a popular watering hole that features an enormous selection of mojitos, a daily happy hour (4pm-7pm), and live acoustic music on the patio at 1pm and 7pm every day.

Farther down Duval stands the inimitable **Sloppy Joe's Bar** (201 Duval St., 305/294-5717, www.sloppyjoes.com, 9am-close daily), which has been luring patrons to the corner of Greene and Duval (supposedly even Ernest Hemingway) since 1937 and is now listed on the National Register of Historic Places. Home to the annual Hemingway Look-Alike Contest, Sloppy Joe's offers terrific food, televised sports, plenty of libations, and live rock, country, or funk music all day long, which often entails three different bands or solo artists from noon to 2am.

Across the street from Sloppy Joe's, the **Rick's/Durty Harry's Entertainment Complex** (202-208 Duval St., 305/296-5513, www.ricksanddurtyharrys.com, 11am-close daily) encompasses eight separate late-night options, including a Mardi Gras-style daiquiri bar, and Durty Harry's, which features several televisions and live rock music 8pm-4am daily. At Duval and Caroline Streets, you'll encounter the clothing-optional **Garden of Eden** atop **The Bull and Whistle Bar** (305/296-4545, www.bullkeywest.com, 10am-4am Mon.-Sat., noon-4am Sun.), where body painting is a frequent activity. **Fat Tuesday Key West** (305 Duval St., 305/296-9373, www.fattuesdaykeywest.com, 10am-close daily) claims to have the world's best selection of frozen drinks, including rumrunners, piña coladas, and New Orleans-style hurricanes.

Also on Duval, **Cowboy Bill's Honky Tony Saloon** (610½ Duval St., 305/295-8219, http://cowboybillskw.blogspot.com, 11am-4am daily) invites you to watch televised sporting events, enjoy a specialty tequila, ride the mechanical bull, or boogie on Key West's largest dance floor.

You can also groove the night away at the predominantly gay **Aqua Nightclub** (711 Duval St., 305/294-0555, www.aquakeywest.com, 2:30pm-3am daily), which features a daily happy hour (2:30pm-8pm) in addition to karaoke, live piano and Caribbean-style music, and drag shows ($15 pp). Not far away lie two more gay hot spots: the **Bourbon St. Pub** (724 Duval St., 305/293-9800, www.bourbonstpub.com, 10am-4am daily), which offers three inner bars, a clothing-optional garden bar, and sexy male dancers, and **801 Bourbon Bar & Cabaret** (801 Duval St., 305/294-4737, www.801bourbon.com, 10am-close daily), which features multiple bars, happy-hour specials (10am-6pm daily), karaoke (6pm Thurs. and Sun.), drag queen bingo (5pm Sun.), and a twice-nightly drag show (9pm and 11pm). Both of these lively complexes factor heavily into annual events like Fantasy Fest and New Year's Eve.

For a less rowdy atmosphere, head to the **Pier House Resort** (1 Duval St., 305/296-4600, www.pierhouse.com), where the **Wine Galley Piano Bar** (6pm-close Fri.-Mon.) offers martini specials and live nightly entertainment on the waterfront. Other enticing hotel options include the weekend cabaret show (9pm Fri.-Sat., $26 pp) at the **La Te Da Hotel** (1125 Duval St., 305/296-6706, www.lateda.com); a full bar inside the **Rambler Lounge** (6:30pm-10pm daily) at the **Casa Marina Resort** (1500 Reynolds St., 305/296-3535, www.casamarinaresort.com); and **Pearl's Patio** (305/293-9805, www.pearlspatio.com, noon-10pm Sun.-Thurs., noon-midnight Fri.-Sat.), the women-only tropical bar at **Pearl's Rainbow** (525 United St., 305/293-9805, www.pearlsrainbow.com) that offers wireless Internet access, a happy hour (5pm-7pm Mon.-Sat.), and special events.

Also off Duval, the **Bottlecap Lounge and Liquor** (1128 Simonton St., 305/296-2807, www.bottlecaplounge.com, noon-4am daily) lures revelers with pool tables, comfortable lounge chairs, oodles of beer, late-night vittles, and live blues and rock music. **Bobby's Monkey Bar** (900 Simonton St., 305/294-2655, noon-4am daily) invites patrons to shoot some pool, play some free Wii games, and try their hand at karaoke (9:30pm Sun.-Mon. and Thurs.-Fri.).

Over on Whitehead, the **Green Parrot Bar** (601 Whitehead St., 305/294-6133, www.greenparrot.com, 10am-4am Mon.-Sat., noon-4am Sun.) has been luring night owls since 1890. Today you'll encounter a daily happy hour (4pm-7pm), an awesome jukebox, and of course, live blues, jazz, rock, and acoustic music almost every night.

Closer to the gulf, you can enjoy live rock and country music, plus a raw bar, at the **Hog's Breath Saloon** (400 Front St., 305/296-4222, www.hogsbreath.com, 10am-2am daily), plus annual events like a bikini contest in October and a Parrot Head tribute party to Jimmy Buffett in November. The **Rum Barrel** (528 Front St., 305/292-7862, www.rumbarrel.com, 11am-1am Mon.-Sat., 11:30am-1am Sun.) provides, as the name implies, a comprehensive

The popular Green Parrot Bar hosts live music almost every night.

rum selection, in addition to live folk, reggae, or classic rock music on an open-air rooftop deck, typically on Thursday, Friday, and Saturday nights.

Captain Tony's Saloon (428 Greene St., 305/294-1838, www.capttonyssaloon.com, 10am-2am Mon.-Sat., noon-2am Sun.), a Key West tradition since 1851 and the original location of Sloppy Joe's from 1933 to 1937, promises, among other things, live contemporary, classic rock, and country music every day, not to mention a glimpse at Ernest Hemingway's former stool. Typically, you can expect solo acoustic performers on weekdays and a house band on the weekend.

Beside the Historic Seaport at Key West Bight, locals flock to the funky **Schooner Wharf Bar** (202 William St., 305/292-3302, www.schoonerwharf.com, 7:30am-4am daily), a weathered, open-air joint that offers excellent seafood, tropical drinks, and live acoustic music three times daily (noon, 7pm, and 9pm). If you haven't had your fill of live entertainment yet, stroll over to the open-air **B.O.'s Fish**

Wagon (801 Caroline St., 305/294-9272, www. bosfishwagon.com, 11am-9pm daily) for the Friday night jam session. Closer to Grinnell, **Dante's** (955 Caroline St., 305/953-5123, www.danteskeywest.com, 11am-10pm daily) features a weekday happy hour (4pm-8pm), daily raw bar specials (4pm-8pm), live entertainment (Thurs.-Sun.), and access to a pool (11am-sunset daily).

You can enjoy some authentic Irish cuisine and live entertainment at **Finnegan's Wake** (320 Grinnell St., 305/293-0222, www.keywestirish.com, 11am-close daily), a lively old-fashioned pub offering an enormous beer, wine, and hot toddies menu. During the peak tourist season, from November to May, you can usually expect Irish music on Friday and Saturday nights, but during the slower summer months, you might encounter local contemporary musicians on a Friday evening. For a more sensual late-night experience, stop by **Better Than Sex** (926 Simonton St., 305/296-8102, www.betterthansexkw.com, 6pm-1am Tues.-Sun. Christmas-Easter, 6pm-1am Wed.-Sun.

Captain Tony's Saloon, site of Hemingway's favorite local watering hole

Apr.-Dec.), an intimate dimly lit bordello-style lounge and restaurant that features live jazz and acoustic music and focuses exclusively on wine and decadent desserts. Even Stock Island has a nightlife option: the casual **Hogfish Bar and Grill** (6810 Front St., 305/293-4041, www.hogfishbar.com, 11am-11pm Mon.-Sat., 9am-11pm Sun.), which provides waterfront views and live blues, rock, and country music on the weekend (Thurs.-Sat.).

THE ARTS
While the rest of the Florida Keys host their fair share of plays, concerts, and screenings, most cultural enthusiasts head first to Key West—and with good reason. Despite its small size, America's Southernmost City nurtures a number of winning theatrical venues and musical organizations.

Theater and Cinema
Situated on the Florida Keys Community College (FKCC) campus, the **Tennessee Williams Theatre** (5901 College Rd., Stock Island, 305/296-1520 or 305/295-7676, www.tennesseewilliamstheatre.com, show times and ticket prices vary) was saved from permanent closure in 2002 by the newly formed, nonprofit Performing Arts Centers for Key West (PACKW). Since then this fantastic venue has featured a variety of nationally recognized performers and productions, from Lily Tomlin's one-woman show to Patti Lupone's musical reviews. To purchase tickets for events at the Tennessee Williams Theatre and other area venues, contact **KeysTix.com** (305/295-7676, http://keystix.ticketforce.com, 10am-2pm Mon.-Fri.).

Mallory Square features the nonprofit **Waterfront Playhouse** (310 Wall St., 305/294-5015, www.waterfrontplayhouse.org, show times and ticket prices vary), home to the Key West Players. From November to May, theater lovers are treated to a variety of cutting-edge productions, from rowdy musical comedies like *Reefer Madness* to classic dramas such as *Twelve Angry Men*.

The Red Barn Theatre (319 Duval St.,

© DANIEL MARTONE

The Red Barn Theatre on Duval Street

305/296-9911 or 866/870-9911, www.redbarn-theatre.com, show times and ticket prices vary) has celebrated live theater for more than three decades. From November to May, the theater showcases a wide array of modern comedies, dramas, and musicals, plus the springtime Short Attention Span Theatre, a well-favored event featuring an assortment of 10-minute plays.

Occasionally, live dance, musical, and theatrical performances take place at the nonprofit **San Carlos Institute** (516 Duval St., www.institutosancarlos.org, show times and ticket prices vary), a stunning multipurpose facility that was founded by Cuban exiles and now features a museum, a library, an art gallery, a school, and a lovely 360-seat theater. Contact the Institute or **KeysTix.com** (305/295-7676, http://keystix.ticketforce.com) for upcoming events.

Even movie lovers won't be disappointed in Key West. The relatively new **Tropic Cinema** (416 Eaton St., 877/761-3456, www.tropic-cinema.com, show times and ticket prices

vary) offers four different screening rooms—the Natella Carper Theater, the Frank Taylor Cinematheque Theater, the George Digital Theater, and the Peggy Dow Theater—and a spacious lobby (dubbed the Sussman Lounge) that have not only played host to the latest independent, alternative, and foreign films, but also community events, from jazz concerts to literary lectures to songwriting festivals. For information about other cultural events in Key West, consult the **Florida Keys Council of the Arts** (1100 Simonton St., 305/295-4369, www.keysarts.com).

Music

If you appreciate live classical music, then you're in luck. For more than 15 years, the **South Florida Symphony Orchestra** (954/522-8445, www.southfloridasymphony.org, show times and ticket prices vary) has offered remarkable performances to the small community of Key West. Now composed of about 90 orchestral musicians and soloists from around the world, the orchestra splits its time between several venues, including the **Tennessee Williams Theatre** (5901 College Rd., Stock Island, 305/296-1520 or 305/295-7676, www.tennesseewilliamstheatre.com) and the **Broward Center for the Performing Arts** (201 SW 5th Ave., Fort Lauderdale, 954/522-5334, www.browardcenter.org).

Typically from October to March, the nonprofit **Key West Pops Orchestra** (305/296-6059, www.keywestpops.org, show times and ticket prices vary) presents operas, Broadway musicals, and other musical performances at the Tennessee Williams Theatre and other area venues. Past shows have included *My Fair Lady, A Little Night Music,* and *The Pajama Game.* Also featured at the Tennessee Williams Theatre is the **FKCC Keys Chorale** (Florida Keys Community College, www.keyschorale.com, show times and ticket prices vary), Monroe County's only major vocal ensemble, which has been performing everything from pop songs to show tunes for more than 20 years. To purchase tickets for all three of these musical organizations, consult **KeysTix.com**

(305/295-7676, http://keystix.ticketforce.com, 10am-2pm Mon.-Fri.).

The **Key West Council on the Arts** has offered **Impromptu Concerts** (www.keywest-impromptu.org, show times and ticket prices vary) for more than 35 years. These concerts, which can range from solo piano performances to brass quintets to world-renowned operas, usually take place at the Tennessee Williams Theatre or at **St. Paul's Episcopal Church** (401 Duval St., 305/296-5142, www.stpauls-keywest.org). For tickets, contact the Tennessee Williams Theatre (305/295-7676).

Another curious option is the **Bahama Village Music Program** (727 Fort St., 305/292-9628, www.bvmpkw.org), a nonprofit group that offers free musical education to the children of Bahama Village, a historical community of multigenerational Bahamian Conchs. The students, who range in age from 6 to 13 and learn various styles of music from piano to percussion, offer free concerts and recitals throughout the year. For more information about musical events in the Key West area, consult the **Florida Keys Council of the Arts** (1100 Simonton St., 305/295-4369, www.key-sarts.com).

FESTIVALS AND EVENTS

Key West may have many facets, but above all, it's still a town that knows how to party. Just consider the numerous festivals and events that lure revelers down here, sometimes even during the hottest months. Beyond fishing tournaments and New Year's Eve bashes, you'll find a number of art and heritage festivals, food events, and other exciting celebrations and competitions throughout the year. Perhaps you can even plan your next trip around such unabashed festivities.

Conch Republic Independence Celebration

On April 23, 1982, the U.S. Border Patrol set up a blockade near Florida City to search for illegal aliens and possible drug runners. Following the subsequent traffic jam on U.S. 1, the people of the Florida Keys briefly declared

their secession from the United States by forming the "Conch Republic," a mock micronation, and successfully ended the disruptive blockade. Since then, for roughly three decades, the people of Key West have honored the 1982 ceremonial secession with the 10-day **Conch Republic Independence Celebration** (www.conchrepublic.com).

Every spring, in late April, residents and visitors can enjoy a lineup of varied activities around the city, such as the raising of the Conch Republic flag at Fort Zachary Taylor Historic State Park and the Great Conch Republic Drag Race, featuring competing drag queens, on Duval Street. Throughout the celebration, you can enjoy an array of events at area bars and restaurants, from the conch shell-blowing contest at the Schooner Wharf Bar to a fiddler's contest at the Green Parrot Bar. Other events include bed and dinghy races, car and crafts shows, miniature golf challenges, a pirate's ball, and of course, the Conch Republic Naval Parade and Great Battle for the Conch Republic—a mock, on-the-water confrontation between the Conch Republic's "armed forces" and the "U.S. Border Patrol," an homage to the April 1982 protest. Needless to say, the Conch Republic is always victorious in the Great Battle that takes place in Key West Bight.

◖ Hemingway Days

The spirit of Ernest Hemingway, one of Key West's most beloved former residents, endures in the Southernmost City—and not just through the popular Ernest Hemingway Home and Museum or because of the numerous establishments, such as Sloppy Joe's Bar and Captain Tony's Saloon, that claim to have been the famous novelist's favorite watering hole. Every summer, in late July, residents and visitors alike celebrate this fascinating man with the annual **Hemingway Days** (800/352-5397, www.hemingwaydays.org), a six-day event that commemorates Hemingway's lust for life; his passion for activities like writing and fishing; his adoration of Key West, where he spent the better part of the 1930s; and of course, his literary works, several of which he wrote while living on this very island.

Scheduled events typically include a literary competition; a Caribbean-style street fair; dramatic performances about Hemingway's life; a museum exhibit of rare Hemingway memorabilia; a three-day marlin tournament; and perhaps most famous, the Hemingway Look-Alike Contest, for which upwards of 150 stocky, white-bearded old men flock to town to demonstrate their uncanny resemblance to this one-of-a-kind American writer. Another not-to-be-missed event is the wacky "Running of the Bulls," a slow-moving parade that features the "Papa" Hemingway look-alikes, dressed in Pamplona-style apparel, including khaki shorts and red berets, and riding or strolling beside phony bulls-on-wheels—a silly photo opportunity for residents and tourists alike.

◖ Fantasy Fest

Every October, tons of revelers pour into Key West for **Fantasy Fest** (1111 12th St., Ste. 211, 305/296-1817, www.fantasyfest.net), a spirited 10-day event that nearly rivals the Big Easy's annual Mardi Gras celebration. With colorful parades, outrageous costumes, and oodles of drag queens, this is surely Key West's grandest—and gayest—party of the year. Initiated in the late 1970s to help the local economy during a traditionally slow period, Fantasy Fest has now become such a successful event that it often sustains the hotels, restaurants, and other local establishments until the winter holiday season. Usually held in late October, culminating with Halloween, this hallowed event features everything from a children's costume contest to a two-day goombay street fair in Bahama Village—essentially, a Bahamian celebration that highlights the calypso-style music and dancing associated with goombay drums. In addition, Fantasy Fest revelers will experience fetish and toga parties, headdress balls, pet masquerades, various costume and wet T-shirt contests, body-painting displays, and plenty of other hedonistic activities. Though not for the faint of heart, Fantasy Fest is indeed a bash worth observing—if not participating in.

© ANDY NEWMAN/FLORIDA KEYS NEWS BUREAU

Costumed revelers frolic during an annual Fantasy Fest parade.

Heritage Festivals

With a past that includes pirate legends, Bahamian immigrants, Civil War skirmishes, Cuban refugees, and other alluring facets, it's little surprise that Key West plays host to a number of cultural events throughout the year. On multiple weekends from late December to mid-March, for instance, those interested in Key West's unique architecture and gardens can take a **Key West House and Garden Tour** ($25 pp) through the historical Old Town district. Sponsored by the **Old Island Restoration Foundation** (322 Duval St., 305/294-9501, www.oirf.org) for the past five decades, these beloved tours allow both residents and visitors a chance to peer beyond the front porches of some of Key West's most one-of-a-kind homes. Each tour features five private domiciles, all of which reflect the varied tastes of their owners and many of which feature authentic restorations, creative renovations, and impressive art and antiques collections.

Meanwhile, in late February, **The Key West Tropical Forest & Botanical Garden** (5210 College Rd., Stock Island, 305/296-1504, www.keywestbotanicalgarden.org) celebrates the island's bountiful flora with **Gardenfest Key West** (prices vary), a three-day event that typically includes raffles, demonstrations, lectures, nature-oriented artwork, and a plant sale, featuring fruit trees, exotic palms, orchids, bromeliads, and native plants. Also in late February, the city celebrates a three-day event known as **Civil War Days** (fees apply for some activities) with candlelit tours of Fort Zachary Taylor (western end of Southard St., 305/292-6713, www.floridastateparks.org/forttaylor), artillery demonstrations, a military parade down Duval Street, and reenacted engagements between Union soldiers and Confederate blockade runners in authentic 19th-century schooners.

In early March, the Old Island Restoration Foundation (322 Duval St., 305/294-9501, www.oirf.org) hosts a popular, one-day **Conch Shell Blowing Contest** (free), also known as the "Conch Honk," during which children, teenagers, adults, and senior citizens alike demonstrate their shell-blowing skills in order to highlight the significance of the conch in Key West's past. Meanwhile, The Key West Tropical Forest & Botanical Garden (5210 College Rd., Stock Island, 305/296-1504, www.keywestbotanicalgarden.org) honors the town's Cuban heritage with **Hot Havana Nights** ($25-30 pp), a single-evening in mid-March displaying Cuban music, dancing, and cuisine.

Typically in late April, music lovers will encounter the curious **Key West Songwriters' Festival** (www.kwswf.com, show times and ticket prices vary), a five-day event that presents more than 30 live concerts at popular locales throughout the city, from the Ocean Key Resort to the San Carlos Institute to Jimmy Buffett's Margaritaville. In late May, residents and visitors celebrate the influence of Cuban culture on the development of Key West with the three-day **Cuban American Heritage Festival** (5570 3rd Ave., 305/295-9665, www.cubanfest.com, prices vary), which typically includes activities like a coast-to-coast conga line, a Latin dance party, a Cuban cigar dinner, a domino tournament, and a progressive dinner at various Cuban restaurants.

Besides Hemingway Days, other popular summertime events include the five-day **Key West Pridefest** (305/294-4603, www.pridefestkeywest.com, fees apply for some activities) in mid-June and the four-day **Mel Fisher Days** (Mel Fisher's Treasures, 200 Greene St., 800/434-1399, www.melfisher.com, fees apply for some activities) in mid-July. In a town that possesses a healthy share of gay-friendly bars and hotels—and whose motto is "one human family"—it's no wonder that Pridefest is a much-anticipated event, filled with contests, shows, tours, dance and cocktail parties, a street fair, and a "pride" parade along Duval Street. A month later, Mel Fisher Days honors a different aspect of the city's heritage—its lust for treasure hunting. To honor the anniversary of Mel Fisher's discovery of the *Atocha* mother lode, this event features, among other activities, a parade, a poker tournament, and a bikini contest that offers authentic treasure coins as prizes.

Later in the year, yet another event highlights the laid-back yet zany vibe of this island paradise. In early November, **Parrot Heads in Paradise, Inc.** (www.phip.com), the nonprofit international organization of Parrot Head Clubs—the official fan clubs of singer-songwriter Jimmy Buffett and the carefree tropical lifestyle he exemplifies—hosts a four-day **Meeting of the Minds** for all members in good standing, whether they be members of the virtual club or one of the more than 200 actual clubs that exist around the world.

Food Events

In a city that celebrates so many hedonistic pleasures, it's no wonder that food plays a major role in so many annual events. Some even focus exclusively on the local cuisine. In mid-January, for instance, the one-day family-friendly **Florida Keys Seafood Festival** (www.fkcfa. org, free) highlights the region's commercial fishing industry by offering the freshest local seafood available, from crab to lobster. Later in January, the four-day **Key West Food & Wine Festival** (800/474-4319, www.keywestfoodandwinefestival.com, prices vary) celebrates an assortment of local delicacies, including seafood, Cuban cuisine, tapas dishes, fine wine, and tropical ice cream at various local bars and restaurants. Other activities may include a coconut bowling tournament and a tea dance at La Te Da.

In mid-April, another annual food extravaganza, the one-day **Taste of Key West** ($1 per food/wine ticket), celebrates the cuisine of more than 100 vineyards and 50 local restaurants while benefiting the efforts of **AIDS Help** (1434 Kennedy Dr., 305/296-6196, www.aidshelp.cc/taste.html). A few months later, in early August, residents and visitors celebrate one of their favorite crustaceans with the **Key West Lobsterfest** (www.keywestlobsterfest. com, prices vary), a three-day event, sponsored by Key West Promotions, Inc. (305/744-9804, www.keywestpromotions.com), that features live music, cold drinks, and naturally, fresh lobster.

Art Festivals

Given how influential Key West's landscape has been on local and visiting musicians, writers, and artists, it seems only natural that the Southernmost City would host its share of art-related events during the peak tourist season. In late January, the long-standing **Key West Craft Show** (305/294-1243, www.keywestartcenter. com/craft.html, prices vary), a two-day juried outdoor craft festival, attracts over 100 potters, fabric experts, jewelry makers, glass sculptors, wood craftsmen, and other skilled artists to Key West's Old Town. For a more unusual experience, consider visiting during **Sculpture Key West** (305/295-3800, www.sculpturekeywest.com, admission fees may apply), an annual wintertime exhibition of contemporary outdoor sculpture throughout the city, namely at attractions like Fort Zachary Taylor Historic State Park, the West Martello Tower, and The Key West Tropical Forest & Botanical Garden. Typically, you can enjoy this event from mid-January to mid-April.

Usually held in late February, the nationally recognized **Old Island Days Art Festival** (305/294-1243, www.keywestartcenter.com/festival.html, prices vary), for well over four decades, has celebrated various art forms amid the historical structures of Key West's Old Town. Originally held as a fundraising event for the building that now houses the **Key West Art Center and Gallery (KWAC)** (301 Front St., 305/294-1241, www.keywestartcenter.com, 10am-5pm daily), this two-day juried, outdoor fine art festival features the work of over 100 painters, photographers, sculptors, and other artists, many of whom definitely favor tropical themes.

Fishing and Racing Events

As in other parts of the Florida Keys, outdoor events are popular in Key West, perhaps none more so than the fishing tournaments and racing championships that take place throughout the year. In late January, thousands of sailors from around the world flock to Key West for the **Key West Race Week** (781/639-9545, www.premiere-racing.com, entry fees apply), a five-day international sailing competition in the waters surrounding the Southernmost City. Beginning in mid-March, men, women, juniors, and young children compete to catch and release more than 40 different fish species in the nine-month-long **Key West Fishing Tournament (KWFT)** (www.keywestfishing-tournament.com, entry fees apply).

In mid-April, elite anglers also compete in the prestigious, five-day **World Sailfish Championship** (866/550-5580, www.world-sailfish.com, entry fees apply), which typically awards cash prizes that total roughly $125,000. From mid-September to early November, celebrities and ordinary fishing enthusiasts come together for the **Redbone Celebrity Tournament Series** (305/664-2002, www.redbone.org, entry fees apply), a trio of three-day "Catch the Cure" competitions throughout the Keys that seek out permit, tarpon, bonefish, and redfish—ultimately benefiting cystic fibrosis research. Also in early November, a slew of high-speed powerboats race across the waters of Key West to vie for the world championship title in the eight-day **Key West World Championship** (www.keywestpowerboatraces.com, entry fees apply)—a competition that's equally appealing to spectators.

Holiday Celebrations

A year in Key West wouldn't be complete without experiencing the city's annual holiday celebrations. In early December, residents and visitors, often dressed in shorts and sandals, line up along Duval Street for the **Key West Holiday Parade** (free), a family-friendly event that usually occurs on a Saturday evening and features decorated floats, marching bands, and perhaps a few Santas holding fishing poles. On a Saturday evening in mid-December, locals "deck the hulls" for the **Key West Lighted Boat Parade** (free), a maritime tradition that features a procession of vessels in Key West Bight. All the boats, most of which are owned by Florida Keys residents, are enhanced by bright lights, holiday decorations, and live music, from choirs to steel drums. Families especially favor this festive event.

For two enchanted evenings in early or mid-December, the self-guided **Holiday Historic Inn Tour** (www.keywestchristmas.org, $20 pp) highlights some of the city's loveliest properties, all of which are decorated for the holiday season with twinkling lights, poinsettia plants, and festooned palm trees. Often you'll be able to step inside such historical inns as the Cypress House, the Curry Mansion, and The Mermaid & The Alligator B&B. In addition, fine food and beverages are usually available throughout the tour.

Not surprisingly, **New Year's Eve** is a popular holiday in the Southernmost City. Among the various midnight celebrations on December 31st, you'll spy a conch shell dropping from the roof of Sloppy Joe's Bar, a pirate wench descending the mast of a schooner at the Historic Seaport, and a local drag queen being lowered from a Duval Street balcony in an enormous, high-heeled shoe. Many of the bars are open into the wee hours, so the celebrating doesn't typically stop at midnight.

Shopping

With its cornucopia of art galleries, gift and souvenir shops, clothing boutiques, jewelry stores, and food emporiums, Key West promises you the most engrossing treasure hunt in the Florida Keys—at least on land. Here shoppers will find all manner of items for sale, from hammocks to erotic literature to pendants fashioned from sunken Spanish coins. While such diverse shopping opportunities exist throughout the city, certain areas such as Mallory Square and the rest of Old Town offer the lion's share of options, especially for tourists.

Naturally, the suggestions listed here merely scratch the surface of Key West's shopping scene. For even more ideas, consult www.shopkeywest.com—or just take a stroll around the neighborhoods.

BAHAMA VILLAGE

Southwest of Whitehead Street and roughly bordered by Southard, Fort, and Louisa Streets lies a historical neighborhood known as **Bahama Village.** Named for its original inhabitants, many of whom were of Bahamian ancestry, this residential area is a lively place in the daytime and rather quiet at night. Some visitors even find it a little too quiet once the sun goes down. In fact, with the occurrence of criminal activities, such as muggings and drug transactions, local police officers often advise outsiders against venturing into this area after dark.

Nevertheless, the presence of several interesting shops and restaurants, such as the dessert-only eatery Better Than Sex, makes Bahama Village an enticing place for tourists. Shoppers might especially appreciate the **Bahama Village Market,** an open-air flea market near the village entrance on Petronia Street. Here you'll find a collection of colorful stalls, featuring typical souvenirs like straw hats, T-shirts, beads, sponges, and Caribbean crafts.

MALLORY SQUARE

Although technically part of Key West's Old Town, **Mallory Square** (1 Whitehead St., www.mallorysquare.com) operates as its own unique entity. Situated at the northernmost part of Duval and Whitehead Streets, this popular collection of shops, eateries, and attractions is perhaps best known for its daily Sunset Celebration, when hundreds of locals and tourists gather beside the shore to enjoy the antics of musicians, artists, acrobats, jugglers, and other street performers, while paying homage to the sun as it seemingly sinks into the Gulf of Mexico.

If you're in search of souvenirs, you're in luck here. Vendor carts present a variety of goods, from coconut pirates to colorful flip-flops. In Mallory Square, you'll also spot the long-standing **Shell Warehouse** (305/294-5168, 8:30am-9pm daily), which offers an intriguing assortment of shells, jewelry, artwork, and decorations. Another favored tourist stop is the **Sponge Market** (305/294-2555, 8am-9pm daily), which features a variety of local art, model ships, sea sponges, shipwreck treasure jewelry, and other maritime collectibles—not to mention an enormous "sponge man," the subject of many a tourist's photograph, just outside the doorway. Not far away, adjacent to Mallory Square, you'll encounter the **Clinton Square Market** (291 Front St., 305/296-6825, 8:30am-6pm daily), an air-conditioned, two-story mall that contains a variety of shops, featuring everything from jewelry and tropical clothing to toys and pet items.

HISTORIC SEAPORT

From Mallory Square, head northeast to the renovated **Historic Seaport** district at Key West Bight, home to dozens of yachts and tour operators. Generally, people come here to hire charters, board sailboats, stroll along the boardwalk, or dine at lively places like the Schooner Wharf Bar, but shoppers will also find a couple

© DANIEL MARTONE

Shoppers may appreciate a stroll through Mallory Square.

of curious stores in the vicinity. Difficult to miss is **Mac's Sea Garden** (208 Margaret St., 305/293-7240, 9am-9pm daily), a rustic gift shop, with chimes hanging beneath the porch roof, an old, weathered pickup sitting in the front yard, and the distinct appearance of a Cajun fishing camp. Not far away, at the corner of Elizabeth and Greene Streets, **Kermit's Key West Key Lime Shoppe** (305/296-0806, www.keylimeshop.com, 9am-9pm daily) offers a whole slew of key lime products, from key lime bath soap to key lime barbecue sauce to classic key lime pie, of course.

OLD TOWN

Although Key West's **Old Town** is generally considered the western half of the island, most of the available shopping opportunities are concentrated on or near **Duval Street,** the main drag of this historical district. Here and on surrounding roads, like Greene and Whitehead Streets, you'll find a ton of places to satisfy your cravings for art, souvenirs, fashion, jewelry, food, and so much more.

Art Galleries

If you're an art lover, then you've come to the right place, for Key West boasts well over 30 art galleries—certainly more than any other place in the Florida Keys. Over half of these can be found on Duval Street, in two separate clusters.

On the upscale end of Duval, closer to the Atlantic Ocean, lie nearly a dozen elegant galleries, bunched together amid tropical foliage and historical buildings. At the **Archeo Gallery** (1208 Duval St., 305/294-3771, www.archeogallery.com, 11am-5pm Tues.-Sat.), you'll find hand-chosen primitive art from around the world, such as vibrant Gabbeh rugs from Iran, teak furniture from Indonesia, and masks, sculpture, pottery, and metalwork from Africa. Across the street stands the **Gingerbread Square Gallery** (1207 Duval St., 305/296-8900, www.gingerbreadsquaregallery.com, 10am-6pm daily), which was established in 1974 by Key West's former mayor Richard Heyman, making it one of the oldest art galleries in town. Represented here are the paintings, sculptures, and glassware of several different

© DANIEL MARTONE

Mac's Sea Garden, near the Historic Seaport

artists, from Sal Salinero's lush rainforest land-scapes to Peter Greenwood's whimsical bubble bottles.

The **Key West Light Gallery** (1203 Duval St., 305/294-0566, www.kwlightgallery.com, 10am-5pm daily) features contemporary photography and paintings that highlight Key West's architecture, explore Cuban culture, and exemplify the concept of light in its many forms. A block down the street, the **Alan S. Maltz Gallery** (1210 Duval St., 305/294-0005, www.alanmaltz.com, 10am-6pm daily) displays the stunning images of Florida's official wildlife photographer.

Several blocks down Duval, closer to the rowdier Gulf of Mexico end, lie nearly 10 more winning galleries, including the **Island Style Gallery** (620 Duval St., 305/292-7800, www.islandstylegalleries.com, 10am-8pm Mon.-Sat., 11am-6pm Sun.), which presents artistic jewelry, handcrafted glass, and colorful, trop-ical-themed home furnishings. On the same side of the street, you'll find the **Guild Hall Gallery** (614 Duval St., 305/296-6076, www.

guildhallgallerykw.com, 10am-8pm daily), which has supported local artists since 1976 and today displays the watercolor and acrylic paintings, contemporary sculpture, and youth-ful jewelry of more than 20 artists. About a block away, you'll enjoy the dramatically il-lumined **Peter Lik Fine Art Photography Gallery** (519 Duval St., 305/292-2550, www. peterlik.com, 10am-9pm daily), one of 13 such galleries in the United States.

Perhaps the most famous gallery in town, however, is the flagship store of **Wyland Galleries** (623 Duval St., 305/292-4998 or 888/292-4998, www.wylandkw.com or www. wylandgalleries.com, 9am-10pm daily), the largest Wyland gallery in the world. Inside this spacious store, you'll see an array of impressive glass creations, bronze sculptures, and vibrant paintings by the prolific muralist and envi-ronmentalist, whose work typically focuses on photogenic marinelife like dolphins, manatees, orcas, and sea turtles. In addition, this incred-ible gallery features the work of Wyland's fellow artists, including David Wight's amazing glass

THE WYLAND WALLS

Robert Wyland, better known simply as Wyland, is indeed the most famous marinelife artist in the world. For more than three decades, Wyland–an avid scuba diver, marine conservationist, painter, sculptor, photographer, and world traveler as well as an official artist for the United States Olympic Committee–has used his artwork to spread awareness about the ocean, its inhabitants, and the need to preserve and protect this fragile environment. His oil and watercolor paintings, bronze and Lucite sculptures, and other creations–which typically feature magnificent whales, peaceful manatees, frisky dolphins, giant sea turtles, and kaleidoscopic tropical fish–are on display in galleries throughout the country, most notably in Florida, California, and Hawaii. He even has two **Wyland Galleries** (www.wylandkw.com) in Key West, including the flagship store (623 Duval St., 305/292-4998) and the one near Mallory Square (102 Duval St., 305/294-5240).

Nicknamed the "Marine Michelangelo" by *USA Today*, Wyland has been recognized for his conservation efforts by the United Nations, the Sierra Club, and other public and private institutions throughout the world. In fact, he cares so deeply about the environment that in 1993 he established the **Wyland Foundation** (www.wylandfoundation.org), a nonprofit organization that has supported numerous art, education, and conservation programs, including his most famous endeavor: the monumental "Wyland Wall" mural project. Begun in 1981 in Laguna Beach, California, this impressive series of 100 life-size marinelife murals now spans 13 countries on five continents, from America to Japan to New Zealand, and captures nearly 1 billion viewers per year. Interestingly, you'll even find several of these amazing murals in southern Florida, including *Minke Whales*, which was created in 1990 at Crane Point's Museum of Natural History in Marathon, as well as a more recent offering, which was painted in October 2012 to replace *Florida's Living Reef* (1993) on the exterior wall of the former Waterfront Market in Key West–both are indeed worth a look. For more information about Wyland's art and conservation efforts, visit www.wylandgalleries.com and www.wyland.com.

wave sculptures. Near Mallory Square, you'll spot another Wyland gallery at 102 Duval Street (305/294-5240 or 888/294-5240, 9am-10pm daily), so be sure to stop there, too.

Of course, there are also plenty of worthwhile art galleries off Duval. Near downtown Key West, the **Audubon House & Tropical Gardens** (205 Whitehead St., 305/294-2116 or 877/294-2470, www.audubonhouse.com, 9:30am-5pm daily) includes the **Audubon House Gallery of Natural History,** which offers a number of limited editions of John James Audubon's famous ornithological paintings from the 19th century. Farther inland, the **Haitian Art Company** (605 Simonton St., 305/296-8932, www.haitian-art-co.com, 10am-7pm daily) sells an array of colorful paintings from Haitian artists like Simeon Michel, who focuses on the verdant Haitian countryside, and Soliman Delva, who strives for social realism. For more information about these and other art galleries, consult the **Florida Keys Council of the Arts** (1100 Simonton St., 305/295-4369, www.keysarts.com).

Gift and Souvenir Shops

Given Key West's supreme popularity among tourists, it surely comes as no surprise that gift and souvenir shops abound in Old Town. For one thing, there's a plethora of strategically placed museum shops in this part of town. In fact, whether they're situated just beyond the front entrance—as with the **Mel Fisher Maritime Museum** (200 Greene St., 305/294-2633, www.melfisher.org, 8:30am-5pm Mon.-Fri., 9:30am-5pm Sat.-Sun.)—or located at the end of the tour, you're usually forced to pass through an eclectic collection of books, DVDs, jewelry, apparel, and the like. If you're interested in less nautically themed items, consider browsing the gift shop at **The Key West Butterfly & Nature Conservatory** (1316 Duval St., 305/296-2988, www.keywestbutterfly.com, 9am-5:30pm daily), which features a wide selection of butterfly-themed jewelry, ceramics, books, and other souvenirs.

You'll find several other curious gift shops along Duval. **KW Hammocks** (717 Duval St., Ste. 2, 305/293-0008, www.kwhammocks.com, hours vary daily), for one, has been distributing hammocks and hammock-style porch swings, chairs, and rockers for over a decade, and while it's true that **Jimmy Buffett's Margaritaville** (500 Duval St., 305/292-1435, www.margaritavillekeywest.com, 9am-11pm daily) is part of a famous bar and restaurant chain, that doesn't mean that the attached store isn't worth browsing. Here you'll find all manner of souvenir hats, T-shirts, flip-flops, lawn chairs, dog collars, and of course, Buffett's novels and CDs. Not far away, you can pick up unique aloe-based fragrances, hair products, and skin creams for women and men at **Key West Aloe** (419 Duval St., 305/517-6365, www.keywestaloe.com, 8:30am-5pm daily). Off Duval, another curious locale is the **Pelican Poop Shoppe** (314 Simonton St., 305/292-9955, www.pelicanpoopshoppe.com, 10am-7pm daily), which presents an array of lamps, weathervanes, metal wall art, and other Caribbean-style crafts. Established in 1976, the **Key West Kite Company** (408 Greene St., 305/296-5483, www.keywestkitecompany.com, 9am-8:30pm daily) provides colorful kites, flags, toys, and yard ornaments to residents and visitors alike.

Now, if you've come to Key West with more amorous amusements in mind, consider stopping by **Fairvilla's Sexy Things** (524 Front St., 305/292-0448, www.fairvilla.com, 9am-midnight daily), where you'll find a wide selection of erotic gifts and games, fantasy fashions, and sensual accessories. Just a few blocks away lies a completely different megastore. With a view of Key West Harbor, the 4,000-square-foot **Saltwater Angler** (243 Front St., 305/294-0700 or 800/223-1629, www.saltwaterangler.com, 9am-8:30pm daily) serves as a one-stop shop for anyone interested in saltwater fishing in the Florida Keys. Operated by Captain Tony Murphy and situated within The Westin Key West Resort & Marina, the Angler houses an extensive inventory of travel and fishing apparel for men and women, plus luggage, wind chimes, stained-glass fish art, rare books, and locally made jewelry. While you're here, you can even ask about fishing guide services.

Clothing and Shoe Boutiques

Most of the clothing and footwear stores in Key West focus on carefree island styles. The **Ron Jon Surf Shop** (503 Front St., 305/293-8880, www.ronjons.com, 9am-9pm daily) is no exception. This two-story behemoth offers a wide array of apparel and accessories for the vacationer, from swimsuits to backpacks to sunglasses. In keeping with that laid-back vibe, **Kino Sandals, Inc.** (107 Fitzpatrick St., 305/294-5044, www.kinosandalfactory.com, 8:30am-5:30pm Mon.-Fri., 9am-5:30pm Sat., 10am-3pm Sun.), established in 1966 by Cuban immigrants, invites visitors to watch the sandals being made by hand, before choosing from an array of men's and women's selections. You can also pick up a pair of sandals at the **Port Sandal Shoppe** (218 Whitehead St., Ste. 2, 305/296-0001, www.sandalshoppe.com, 9:30am-7:30pm daily), which houses thousands of different styles from popular brands like Teva, Timberland, and Crocs. For a real island look, consider stopping by **Hair Wraps of Key West** (310 Duval St., 305/293-1133, www.hairwrapsofkeywest.com, 10am-10pm daily) and let the staff adorn your hair with braids, corn rows, and beads. Henna tattoos, charms, and hair accessories are also available.

For fancier duds, visit **Evan & Elle** (725 Duval St., 305/296-4617, www.shopbiton.com, 10am-3pm Mon.-Fri., longer hours Nov.-Apr.), which offers upscale clothing for men and women, ideal for those headed out on a cruise. Off Duval, the stylish **Blue Boutique** (718 Caroline St., 305/292-5172, www.blueislandstore.com, 10am-6pm daily) features high-end, contemporary fashions from today's hottest designers, such as Nicole Miller and James Perse.

If you want to match your new outfit with the perfect hat, purse, or necklace, stroll to The Westin Key West Resort & Marina, where the locally owned **Key West Madhatter** (253 Front St., 305/294-1364 or 888/442-4287, www. kw-madhatter.com, 9am-11pm daily) offers, among other accessories, more than 2,000 hats for women, men, and children, from elegant straw hats to goofy holiday fedoras.

Jewelry Stores

You'll certainly find an impressive assortment of shiny, pretty things in Key West, including oodles of gemstones at **Diamonds International** (122 Duval St., 305/293-1111, www.shopdi.com, 11am-9pm daily), the largest duty-free jeweler in the world, as well as emerald, conch pearl, and Australian black opal rings at **Emeralds International** (104 Duval St., 305/294-2060 or 877/689-6647, www.emeraldsinternational.com, 10am-6pm daily). For more precious gemstones—plus Key West's largest supply of Swiss watches—head to **Little Switzerland** (423 Front St., 248/809-5560, ext. 20360, www.littleswitzerland.com, 9am-5pm daily). If your interests run a little less expensive, visit **Local Color** (276 Margaret St., 305/292-3635, www.localcolorkeywest. com, 9am-10pm daily), which since 1988 has offered a wide array of fun jewelry, including locally inspired beads and charms, Happy Hour rings, and silver and gold "KW" hook bracelets. You could also try **Paradise Tattoo** (627 Duval St., 305/292-9110, www.paradis-etattoo.com, 10am-10pm daily), which offers basic jewelry in addition to tattoo and body-piercing services.

For valuables that will evoke memories of your trip to the Florida Keys, head to **Mel Fisher's Treasures** (200 Greene St., 305/296-9936 or 800/434-1399, www.melfisher.com, 9:30am-5pm daily), situated at the rear of the Mel Fisher Maritime Museum. Here you can purchase a piece of the famous *Nuestra Señora de Atocha* shipwreck, including pearls, iron spikes, musket balls, pieces of eight, and pendants and earrings crafted from old Spanish coins. In addition, you can speak with the staff

about investing in the site—from which underwater explorers are still recovering hidden coins, artifacts, and other treasures. Just be prepared to spend a bundle. Being an investor isn't cheap, but neither are the goods in the store, where you might spot an encrusted mystery object with a tiny embedded emerald on sale for $19,999.

Food and Beverage Emporiums

Key West residents celebrate all aspects of life, not the least of which is fine food. If you're hoping to take a taste of the Conch Republic home with you, look no farther than the **Key West Key Lime Pie Co.** (511 Greene St., 305/517-6720, www.keywestkeylimepieco.com, 10am-6pm Mon.-Sat., noon-5pm Sun.), which sells award-winning key lime pies in addition to gourmet jellies, marinades, cookies, candies, spices, cookbooks, and other items, including the popular key lime pie bar—a scrumptious treat that features a slice of key lime pie covered in rich chocolate.

Of course, key lime pie isn't all that Key West has to offer. Founded by Cuban immigrant and cigar maker Fausto Castillo, **Fausto's Food Palace** (www.faustos.com) has served the people of Key West with fine wines, gourmet cheeses, and other delicious vittles since 1926. Today Fausto's, which has moved and expanded over the years, offers two locations: 522 Fleming Street (305/296-5663, 8am-8pm Mon.-Sat., 8am-7pm Sun.) and 1105 White Street (305/294-5221, 8am-8pm Mon.-Sat., 8am-7pm Sun.). Wine lovers might also appreciate **The Key West Winery** (103 Simonton St., 305/292-1717 or 866/880-1717, www.thekeywestwinery.com, 10am-6pm Mon.-Sat., noon-6pm Sun.), which features unusual key lime, mango, and other tropical wines, plus a variety of key lime condiments. Another option is the **Cork & Stogie** (1218 Duval St., 305/517-6419, www.corkandstogie.com, 10am-11pm daily), which offers a fine selection of wine and cigars, including those produced by **The Original Key West Cigar Factory** (305/517-7273, www.kw-cigarfactory.com), whose history stretches back to the 1880s.

Sports and Recreation

GOLF

While the Florida Keys archipelago isn't the golf mecca that other parts of the Sunshine State purport to be, that doesn't mean that golfers are without options. Besides private golf courses like those at the Ocean Reef Club in Key Largo and the Sombrero Country Club in Marathon, golfers will find a lovely, palm-studded golf course in the Lower Keys. Encompassing at least a third of Stock Island, the 200-acre **Key West Golf Club** (6450 E. College Rd., 305/294-5232, www.keywestgolf. com, $50-95 with a cart) features an 18-hole, 6,500-yard public golf course, set on the gulf side of U.S. 1, amid dense mangroves, tranquil lakes, varied wildlife, and the ever-present trade winds. This year-round full-service facility—incidentally, the southernmost golf course in the continental United States—also offers a driving range ($8 per bucket), rental clubs ($40 per set), bag storage ($125 yearly), locker rentals ($80 yearly), a pro golf shop and clubhouse, a golf instruction ($410-710 per class), and private parking.

⚡ BIKING

Whether you're an experienced or novice rider, Key West is a lovely, welcoming place to traverse by bicycle. Just remember that you'll have to share the streets with cars and other vehicles, so take care while you tour the neighborhoods—and wear a proper helmet at all times. Bicycles can be rented from several different outfitters, including **Eaton Bikes** (830 Eaton St., 305/294-8188, www.eatonbikes.com, 9am-6pm Mon.-Sat., 9am-4pm Sun., $12-45 daily, $40-135 weekly), which offers a range of bicycles, from trikes to mountain bikes to tandems, plus free delivery and pickup service throughout Key West. **The Bike Shop of Key West** (1110 Truman Ave., 305/294-1073, www.thebikeshopkeywest.com, 9am-6pm Mon.-Sat., 10am-4pm Sun., $12 daily, $60 weekly, $180 monthly), the oldest in town, also provides a

wide array of bicycles, plus accessories, bicycle sales, and a service/repair department. All rentals include locks, lights, baskets, and wide soft seats.

Another helpful source for bicycle rentals is **Adventure Rentals** (305/293-8883, www. keywest-scooter.com, 9am-5pm daily, $8 for four hours, $15 daily, $60 weekly), which features multiple locations—at 0 Duval Street, 617 Front Street, 135 Simonton Street, and Cruise Ship Pier B—and also offers scooters ($30 for four hours, $50 daily), Harley motorcycles (starting from $203 for four hours, $268 daily, $935 weekly), and multiple-passenger electric cars ($94-137 per two hours, $159-202 daily). In addition, **A&M Rentals** (305/896-1921, www.amscooterskeywest. com, 8am-8pm daily, $15 daily, $85 weekly) features three spots from which to rent kid-size bicycles, cruisers, and tandems: 523 Truman Avenue, 513 South Street, and 500 Truman Avenue. You can also rent one-seater scooters ($35 daily, $109 weekly), two-seater scooters ($55 daily, $179 weekly), and multi-seater electric cars ($99 daily)—all popular ways to get around town. Free customer pickup and drop-off services are available.

Even Stock Island has a bicycle outfitter. Just north of the Hurricane Hole Marina, **Re-Cycle** (5160 Overseas Hwy., Stock Island, 305/292-3336 or 305/294-7433, www.recyclekw.com, 9am-9pm daily, $18 daily, $65 weekly) offers a full-service shop and free delivery for its wide array of bicycles, so you'll find no shortage of ways to enjoy a ride around this lovely city.

FISHING AND BOATING

Anglers come from all over the world to explore the waters surrounding Key West, a place that boasts year-round fishing opportunities. Every month, several different fish species are in season, and anglers can choose from a variety of fishing locales, including deep harbors, backcountry flats, coral reefs, and offshore waters.

No wonder Ernest Hemingway found fishing down here so appealing.

For a small city, Key West sure does have an impressive number of marinas, from the **Historic Seaport at Key West Bight** (305/295-9225, www.seaportrealtorskeywest. com) near Old Town to the **Hurricane Hole Marina** (5130 Overseas Hwy., 305/294-8025, www.hurricaneholekeywest.com) on adjacent Stock Island. In fact, Stock Island features several marinas, including the deepwater **Old Island Harbor** (7009 Shrimp Rd., 305/294-2288, www.oldislandharbor.com) and the nostalgic **Safe Harbour Marina** (6810 Front St., 305/294-9797, www.safeharbourmarina.com). So if you're planning to bring your own boat in order to fish the abundant backcountry and offshore waters of the Florida Keys, you'll find no shortage of boat slips and marine services in the area.

Most anglers come to Key West with sportfishing charters in mind, and here, too, you'll find no scarcity of options. At the **Key West City Marina at the Garrison Bight** (1801 N. Roosevelt Blvd., 305/809-3981, www.keywestcity.com), for instance, you can hire any number of boats from Charter Boat Row, including offshore fishing services like **Fishcheck Key West Fishing Charters** (Slip #1, 305/295-0484 or 877/434-7459, www.fishcheckcharters.com, $165-750 per half day, $200-900 for six hours, $250-1,100 daily) and **Wild Bill Sportfishing** (305/296-2533 or 305/744-7957, www.wildbillkeywest.com, $150-650 per half day, $185-750 for six hours, $225-900 daily), both of which offer individual seats as well as private charters for up to six passengers. Among the other deep-sea fishing vessels docked at the City Marina, you'll spot the *Ramerezi* (305/294-0803 or 305/745-2789, www.ramerezi.com, $450 per half day, $900 daily) and the **Charter Boats *Linda D.*** (Slips #19 and #20, 305/296-9798 or 800/299-9798, www.charterboatlindad.com, $600-675 per half day, $900-975 daily), all of which are helmed by longtime local fishing captains and can accommodate up to six anglers at a time.

If you're interested in shallow-water flats fishing and saltwater fly-fishing, consider **Almost There! Sportfishing Charters** (5001 5th Ave., Stock Island, 305/295-9444 or 800/795-9448, www.almostthere.net, $450 per half day, $750 daily), Key West's largest charter company, or as an alternative, **Sting Rea Charters** (305/744-0903, www.flyfishingthekeys.com, $400 per half day, $600 daily), which transports its vessel from Sugarloaf Key to various locations and leads anglers to the waters around the Lower Keys and the Marquesas in search of tarpon, barracuda, permit, and bonefish. For reef and wreck fishing, among other fishing styles, consult **Mean Green Charters** (Murray Marina, 5710 Overseas Hwy., Stock Island, 305/304-1922, www.meangreenfishing.com, $600 per half day, $900 daily), **Cheerio Charters** (Hurricane Hole Marina, 5130 Overseas Hwy., Stock Island, 305/797-6446, www.cheeriocharters.com, $600 per half day, $900 daily), or **Boo-Ya Charters** (Charter Boat Row, 1801 N. Roosevelt Blvd., 305/292-6692, www.booyakeywest.com, $600 per half day, $800 daily), through which you'll possibly snag grouper, snapper, amberjack, kingfish, tuna, barracuda, permit, yellowtail, cobia, and sharks. Families may especially appreciate **No Worries Charters** (711 Eisenhower Dr., 305/393-2402, www.noworriescharters.com, $500-600 per half day, $800-900 daily), a company based in the Key West City Marina that allows pets on board; supports catch-and-release fishing, especially for children; and customizes trips to include boating, snorkeling, dolphin-watching, and light-tackle fishing. Rates are often negotiable.

In general, fishing trips are offered daily, and rates, which typically include bait, tackle, ice, and proper fishing licenses, are for the entire trip, not per angler. For most fishing charters, reservations are recommended and deposits are often required. Also, cancellation policies vary between operators, so be sure to check such details well in advance, or else you may lose your deposit.

As an alternative to bringing your own boat or hiring a fishing charter, you can always rent a seaworthy vessel from **Sunset**

Watersports Key West (Hurricane Hole Marina, 5130 Overseas Hwy., Stock Island, 305/294-5500, www.sunsetwatersports.info, 9am-6pm daily), which offers a range of vessels, from 17-foot fishing boats ($250 per half day, $325 daily) to 24-foot pontoons ($400 per half day, $500 daily). Boats come equipped with GPS, fish and depth finders, live bait wells, and bimini tops.

If you need to rent a fishing rod or stock up on essentials like live bait and cold beer, head first to the Historic Seaport district, where **Key West Bait & Tackle** (241 Margaret St., 305/292-1961, www.keywestbaitandtackle. com, 7am-7pm daily) features a wide selection of fishing tackle, rods and reels, frozen bait, lures, hooks, sunglasses, towels, and other necessities. Other helpful fishing stores include **The Angling Company** (333 Simonton St., 305/292-6306, www.theanglingcompany.com, 9:30am-7pm daily) and the **Saltwater Angler** (243 Front St., 305/294-3248 or 800/223-1629, www.saltwaterangler.com, 9am-8:30pm daily), a one-stop shop for travel gear, fishing apparel, reels, rods, sunglasses, and other fishing accessories.

As a bonus, all three stores can help you arrange fishing charters. Through Key West Bait & Tackle, you can opt for a backcountry flats fishing charter ($450 per half day, $550 for six hours, $650 daily) in search of redfish, snook, permit, and bonefish; a deep-sea fishing excursion ($800 per half day, $950 for six hours, $1,200 daily) to snag tuna, wahoo, mahimahi, and other game fish; and a light-tackle saltwater fishing charter ($750 per half day, $850 for six hours, $950 daily), which allows you to fish for tarpon in the harbor, marlin and swordfish in the offshore waters, and yellowtail near the reefs. Through The Angling Company and Saltwater Angler, you'll also find a slew of professional guides (rates vary) for flats fishing, offshore fishing, and light-tackle fishing.

KAYAKING

Paddling enthusiasts will find a number of helpful operators in Key West. Based at the

Hurricane Hole Marina, **Lazy Dog** (5130 Overseas Hwy., Stock Island, 305/295-9898, www.lazydog.com, 9am-5pm daily) offers two-hour guided kayaking tours ($40 pp) through backcountry waters and winding mangrove creeks. Lazy Dog also features a four-hour kayaking and snorkeling trip ($60 pp) along the Mosquito Coast, plus single and double kayak rentals ($25 per half day, $35 daily), stand-up paddleboard rentals ($30 each), paddleboard tours ($40 pp), and paddleboard yoga ($30 pp). Reservations are required, and complimentary pickups are available. Area maps are provided with all rentals.

Similarly, **Blue Planet Kayak** (305/294-8087 or 800/979-3370, www.blue-planet-kayak.com) offers guided kayaking trips into the fascinating backcountry, such as the 2.5-hour Boca Chica Tour (10am and 12:40pm in winter, 10am and 3pm in summer, $50 pp) and the 2.5-hour Romantic Sunset & Moonlight Tour ($50 pp). Beginners and families are welcome, though advance reservations are required. Since tour guides will only lead a maximum of 10 passengers on each personalized trip, slots can fill up quickly. Complimentary transportation is available for all tour customers. In addition, Blue Planet provides rentals for sit-in single kayaks ($30 per half day, $40 daily), tandem kayaks ($40 per half day, $50 daily), and fishing kayaks ($30 per half day, $40 daily). For the fishing kayaks, only charts, anchors, and advice are included; anglers must bring their own tackle.

For an alternative experience, consider **Key West Eco Tours** (305/290-2047, www.key-westecotours.com), situated in the Historic Seaport at Key West Bight, behind the Turtle Kraals Restaurant and Bar at the end of Margaret Street. As part of a 4.5-hour ecotour ($99 adults, $79 children under 13) that includes sailing and coral reef snorkeling, Key West Eco Tours offers kayaking trips amid seagrass beds and winding mangrove creeks, where you'll get an up-close look at tropical fish, aquatic birds, sea turtles, spotted eagle rays, dolphins, crabs, sponges, and other marine wonders. Tours occur twice daily

BOATING SAFETY

On especially gorgeous days, you're likely to see a number of powerboats, sailboats, yachts, kayaks, and other vessels in the offshore waters extending from Miami to the Dry Tortugas. With so much action, there's bound to be chaos—unless, of course, boaters obey the following safety guidelines, for the sake of themselves as well as their passengers.

- **Verify Vessel Safety:** Before heading out on the water, make sure that your vessel has been properly maintained, that it meets all local and state regulations, and that your registration numbers are displayed prominently.

- **Equip Yourself:** When planning a boating trip, double-check that you have the following items on board: proper vessel documentation and insurance information, nautical charts, a marine radio, an anchor, a first-aid kit, mounted fire extinguishers, navigation lights, visual distress signals, sound-producing devices, a marine sanitation device, drinking water, extra fuel, and enough personal flotation devices (PFDs) for you and all your passengers.

- **Wear Your Life Jacket:** While it might seem more liberating to ride, fish, or kayak without a PFD, it's imperative that you actually wear one at all times. Not all boating accidents occur in bad weather and rough seas; many happen in shallow water on deceptively calm, clear days, so be sure to wear a life jacket—even a lightweight, inflatable one—whenever you're on the water.

- **Stay Safe and Sober:** Although many boaters will partake of beer and other alcoholic beverages while out on the water, it's simply not advisable to do so. Wind, noise, motion, and sunlight can intensify the effects of alcohol and prescription medications, making it exceedingly dangerous to operate a vessel while under the influence.

- **Monitor Your Propeller:** Unfortunately, boat propellers are responsible for numerous injuries and fatalities every year. To avoid being yet another statistic, purchase propeller safety devices such as sensors and propeller guards, and don't forget to wear an engine cut-off lanyard at all times—which will ensure that if you and, by extension, your lanyard are thrown from the boat, the engine will immediately power down.

- **Monitor Your Passengers:** To ensure your passengers' safety, never allow them to board or disembark while the engine is running, and insist that they remain seated (in proper seats and not on the bow or transom) while the boat is in motion. In an effort to avoid accidents, assign someone to keep watch around the propeller area whenever other passengers, especially children, are swimming in the surrounding waters. To protect the passengers of other boats, stay alert when operating in congested areas, avoid swimmers altogether, and be aware of boats that are towing skiers or tubers. If someone on your vessel falls overboard, stop immediately, turn the boat around, keep the person in sight as you approach, and shut the engine off before rescuing him or her.

For additional advice or information about boating safety courses, consult the **Boat Owners Association of The United States (BoatU.S.)** (800/395-2628, www.boatus.com) or the **U.S. Coast Guard's Boating Safety Division** (www.uscgboating.org), which aims to prevent fatalities, injuries, and property damage on U.S. waterways by improving the knowledge and skills of recreational boaters.

(9am-1:30pm year-round, 2pm-sunset in winter, 3:30pm-sunset in summer) and allow a maximum of six passengers. Double-seat, sit-on-top kayaks are provided.

Based out of The Westin Key West Resort & Marina at 245 Front Street, **Danger Charters** (305/304-7999 or 305/296-3272, www.dangercharters.com) operates daily sailing excursions amid pristine coral reefs, deserted mangrove islands, and sponge gardens in the backcountry. These half-day (9:30am, $75 pp) and full-day trips (10:30am, $100 pp) also feature kayaking and snorkeling and include snacks, beverages, and gear.

DIVING AND SNORKELING

Like the rest of the Florida Keys, Key West is surrounded by thriving coral reefs and fascinating shipwrecks. On your own, you can easily dive and snorkel amid the tropical fish and varied coral formations in the bountiful waters near **Fort Zachary Taylor Historic State Park** (western end of Southard St., 305/292-6713 or 305/295-0037, www.floridastateparks.org/forttaylor or www.fortzacharytaylor.com, 8am-sunset daily, $7 vehicles with 2-8 passengers plus $0.50 pp, $4.50 motorcycles and single-occupant vehicles, $2.50 pedestrians, bikers, and extra passengers) and the **Dry Tortugas National Park** (305/242-7700, www.nps.gov/drto/index.htm or www.dry.tortugas.national-park.com, sunrise-sunset daily, $5 weekly), roughly 68 miles to the west. Still, many of the underwater attractions this far south are only accessible through professional diving charters.

Besides offering scuba-diving instruction and equipment rentals, several local companies, such as **Southpoint Divers** (610 Front St., 800/891-3483, www.southpointdivers.com, 8:30am-noon and 1:30pm-5pm daily), provide trips to two curious wrecks: the 187-foot *Cayman Salvage Master* ($85-120 pp) and the 522-foot **USNS** *General Hoyt S. Vandenberg* ($115-150 pp), a former troop transport ship during World War II, later the backdrop for the film *Virus,* and now the foundation for an artificial reef. Sunk in May 2009, the ship has since become a habitat for varied fish and offers a unique look at the developing stages of coral growth. Guides are required for all open water dives on the *Vandenberg.* Varied gear—including tanks, weights, regulators, wetsuits, and nitrox bottles—is available through Southpoint Divers, and classes range from a refresher course ($75 pp) to a PADI dive master course ($895 pp).

In addition to leading excursions to the Cayman and *Vandenberg* wrecks, the **Subtropic Dive Center** (1605 N. Roosevelt Blvd., 305/296-9914 or 800/853-3483, www.subtropic.com, 8:30am-12:30pm and 1:30pm-6pm daily, $80-150 pp) and **Dive Key West** (3128 N. Roosevelt Blvd., 305/296-3823 or

Divers explore the USNS *General Hoyt S. Vandenberg,* an artificial reef near Key West.

800/426-0707, www.divekeywest.com, 9am-1pm and 2pm-6pm daily, $75-164 pp)—one of the oldest and largest full-service diving facilities in the Florida Keys—each offer trips to other wrecks, such as **Joe's Tug,** a storm-battered vessel that sits in 65 feet of water and is now home to assorted coral formations and nosy eels.

Additional diving resources include **Lost Reef Adventures** (261 Margaret St., 305/296-9737 or 800/952-2749, www.lostreefadventures.com, 9am-1pm and 1:30pm-5:30pm daily, $65-180 pp) and the **Captain's Corner Dive Center** (125 Ann St., 305/296-8865 or 305/304-0437, 9:30am-1:15pm and 2pm-5:30pm daily, $65-130 pp), whose 60-foot, aluminum diving vessel was used in the film *Licence to Kill.* Some of these operators even offer night dives as well as trips to reef formations like the deep, spur-and-groove networks of **Sand Key, Rock Key,** the **Eastern Dry Rocks,** and the **Western Sambo Ecological Reserve.** Other curious habitats include the **Kedge Ledge,** a patch reef that contains coral-encrusted anchors from 18th-century schooners, and the **Ten-Fathom Ledge,** a series of coral ledges, caves, and outcroppings that nurture grouper, lobster, sharks, and eagle rays.

Like the rest of the Keys, Key West appeals to snorkelers, too. In fact, all of the aforementioned diving operators also cater to snorkelers, offering at least two trips daily ($40-50 adults, $35-45 children), with rental equipment usually included in the price. In addition, **Sebago Watersports** (201 William St., 305/292-4768 or 800/507-9955, www.keywestsebago.com, 9am-12:30pm and 1pm-4:30pm daily, $49 adults, $25 children), **Sunset Watersports Key West** (201 William St., 305/296-2554, www.sunsetwatersportskeywest.com, times vary daily, $35-40 adults, $25 children 6-11, free for children under 6), and **Fury Water Adventures** (1 Duval St. and 245 Front St., 305/294-8899 or 877/994-8898, www.furycat.com, 9:30am-12:30pm and 1pm-4pm daily, $40 adults, $20 children 6-12) offer snorkeling trips, among other water-related activities. Instruction and necessary equipment are provided with all trips. Based out of the Historic Seaport at Key West Bight, **Sunny Days** (866/878-2223, www.sunnydayskeywest.com), operated by Fury Water Adventures, also features the *Fast Cat* (305/296-5556 or 800/236-7937, 8am-5pm daily, $140 adults, $70 children 6-12, free for children under 6, plus $5 park entrance fee for guests 17 and over), a high-speed catamaran that can whisk you to the waters surrounding Dry Tortugas National Park for some incredible snorkeling opportunities.

Two other noteworthy vessels, the *Echo* catamaran (Historic Seaport at Key West Bight, 305/292-5044, www.dolphinecho.com, 9am-1pm and 1:30pm-5:30pm daily, $74-89 pp) and the smaller *Amazing Grace* (6000 Peninsula Ave., Stock Island, 305/294-5026 or 800/593-6574, www.wildaboutdolphins.com, 8am-noon and 1pm-5pm daily, $95 pp), combine snorkeling trips with wild dolphin encounters. Both offer private charters as well.

You might also want to visit **Snuba of Key West** (Key West City Marina at the Garrison Bight, 1801 N. Roosevelt Blvd., 305/292-4616, www.snubakeywest.com, 9am, 1pm, and 4pm daily, $99 adults, $79 children 8-12, $44 riders or non-Snuba snorkelers), where you can try an unusual form of deepwater snorkeling that requires no dive certification. On these personal guided tours amid the offshore coral reefs, you'll be able to breathe easily underwater without wearing heavy, restrictive diving gear. Just note that children must be at least 8 years old to try Snuba snorkeling.

Though nearly all of the aforementioned diving and snorkeling outfitters should have the equipment and accessories that you need, you can also make a quick stop at **Divers Direct** (535 Greene St., 305/293-5122, www.diversdirect.com, 9am-7pm Mon.-Thurs., 9am-8pm Fri.-Sat., 10am-7pm Sun.), a well-stocked scuba-diving retailer, for any last-minute items.

OTHER OUTDOOR ACTIVITIES

For thrills of a different kind, consider heading to the Sunset Marina, where you can board the year-round **White Knuckle Thrill Boat Ride**

(5555 College Rd., Stock Island, 305/797-0459, www.whiteknucklethrillboatride.com, $59 pp), an exhilarating, wet-and-wild jet boat experience that features twists, slides, and 360-degree spins in the waters near Key West. If you'd prefer to be in control of your own white-knuckle experience, feel free to rent a Jet Ski, Sea-Doo, or WaveRunner from the following outfitters: **Barefoot Billy's** (The Reach Resort, 1435 Simonton St., 305/849-0815, www.barefootbillys.com, 9am-6pm daily, $70 per half hour, $100 hourly), **Island Water Sports** (The Westin Key West Resort & Marina, 245 Front St., 305/296-1754, www.islandwatersports.us, 9am-sunset daily, $75 per half hour, $100 hourly, $10 per extra passenger), or **Key West Water Tours** (Hurricane Hole Marina, 5106 Overseas Hwy., Stock Island, 305/294-6790, www.keywestwatertours.com, $99 hourly). In addition, all three operators offer guided two-hour tours around the island of Key West every day. Billy's tour times include 10am ($99 pp), 12:30pm ($125 pp), and 3:30pm ($125 pp), while Island Water Sports leaves at 9:30am, 11:30am, 1:30pm, 3:30pm, and 5:30pm ($125 pp, $10 per extra passenger). Key West Water Tours, meanwhile, leads tours at 10am, 12:30pm, 3:30pm, and sunset ($135-155 pp).

Now, if you'd rather be *above* the water, you can always opt for a parasailing adventure. Three such companies operate out of the Historic Seaport at Key West Bight: **ParaWest Parasailing** (700 Front St., 305/292-5199, www.parawestparasailing.com, 9am-6pm daily, $30 pp for morning rides, $45 single riders, $75 double riders, $110 triple riders), **Sebago Watersports** (201 William St., 305/292-4768 or 800/507-9955, www.keywestsebago.com, 9am-4pm daily in winter, 10am-5pm daily in summer, $55 single riders, $85 tandem riders), and **Sunset Watersports Key West** (201 William St., 305/296-2554, www.sunsetwatersportskeywest.com, 9am-6pm daily, $39 pp), which also operates out of Smathers Beach. Another operator, **Fury Water Adventures** (305/294-8899 or 877/994-8898, www.furycat.com, 9am-6pm daily, $40 pp), offers parasailing adventures from two locations:

the Pier House Resort (1 Duval St.) and The Westin Key West Resort & Marina (245 Front St.). All four offer solo and tandem rides, and all promise smooth take-offs, gentle landings, breathtaking aerial views, and safe experiences. No matter which you choose, try to book your trip in advance, especially during the peak winter months.

For a combination of such activities, consider opting for Fury's **Ultimate Adventure** (10am-4pm daily, $139 adults, $70 children 6-12, free for children under 6), an all-inclusive experience that features kayaking, reef snorkeling, Jet Skiing, parasailing, rock climbing, and access to a water trampoline, plus a complimentary meal and unlimited beverages. Sunset Watersports offers a similar package, the **"Do It All!" Party Boat Adventure** (10am-4pm daily, $129 adults, $59 seniors and children under 10), which includes snorkeling, kayaking, rafting, sunfish sailing, knee-boarding, waterskiing, windsurfing, and access to various water sports, plus a grilled lunch. Not to be outdone, Sebago Watersports features its own version of this all-day fun with the **Power Adventure** (10am-4pm daily, $149 adults, $75 children), which encompasses reef snorkeling, a guided kayaking tour, parasailing, and access to personal watercraft, water trampolines, and other water sports—plus free meals, snacks, and beverages. For all three adventures, booking online will typically save you a bit of money.

◀ SPAS AND YOGA

What better way to relax after a hard day of golfing, biking, fishing, kayaking, diving, or parasailing than to experience a soothing massage treatment or beachside yoga lesson. Fortunately, Key West provides an array of such rejuvenating experiences.

Several area resorts, in fact, feature on-site spas. At the **Pier House Resort** (1 Duval St., 305/296-4600, www.pierhouse.com), the full-service **Caribbean Spa** (8:30am-7pm daily) offers manicures ($35 pp), pedicures ($40-70 pp), restorative facials ($65-165 pp), tanning services ($60-140 pp), and moisturizing body treatments ($115 pp), such as the full-body detoxifying mud wrap. Several massages ($70-170 pp) are also available, including the 80-minute hot stone therapy massage and the 80-minute, head-to-toe Caribbean Spa Coma, which proves to be as mind-numbing as it sounds. Guests should reserve appointments in advance and provide at least four hours' notice for any cancellations.

Meanwhile, the adjacent **Ocean Key Resort & Spa** (0 Duval St., 305/296-7701 or 800/328-9815, www.oceankey.com) features the waterfront **SpaTerre** (305/295-7017, 9am-6pm daily), which provides day spa services as well as spa vacation packages. At SpaTerre, men and women alike can experience various massages ($65-175 pp), refreshing body treatments ($70-110 pp), such as the Caribbean Seaweed Body Mask, and incredible Balinese and Thai spa rituals ($165-230 pp), such as the Javanese Royal Spa Treatment, which includes a Balinese spa massage, an herbal exfoliation, a cool yogurt splash, an aromatic shower, and a tub soaking amid rose petals and tropical fragrances. Face and body depilation (rates vary), facials ($60-150 pp), manicures ($20-50 pp), and pedicures ($20-100 pp), including the ultra-special Key Lime Margarita Pedicure, are also available. An adjacent fitness center even offers yoga classes and a stretching patio.

At **Southernmost on the Beach** (508 South St., 305/296-6577, www.southernmostresorts.com), the full-service **Paradise Day Spa** (305/879-7352, www.keywestparadiseday spa.com, 9am-9pm daily) offers an array of salon and spa services. Here hotel guests as well as nonguests can enjoy various manicures ($40-60 pp), pedicures ($50-100 pp), facials ($80-150 pp), massages ($50-130 pp), and body wraps and treatments ($100-150 pp). Other salon services, such as waxing ($20-100 pp) and electrolysis ($30-300 pp), are also available. As with most spas, appointment cancellations must be made 24 hours in advance.

Another top-notch spa can be found at the **Casa Marina Resort** (1500 Reynolds St., 888/303-5717, www.casamarinaresort.com). Only open to hotel guests at the Casa Marina and its sister facility, **The Reach Resort** (1435

Simonton St., 888/318-4316, www.reachresort. com), the **Spa al Mare** presents facials ($100-160 pp), massages ($60-180 pp), aromatherapy treatments ($100-210 pp), and yoga classes ($20-80 pp). Spa packages are also available. Note that all massages are offered either in the studio or on the beach, and bear in mind that guests must notify the spa 24 hours in advance to cancel an appointment.

Beyond luxurious resorts, Key West also contains several stand-alone day spas. The locally owned **Prana Spa** (625 Whitehead St., 305/295-0100, www.pranaspakeywest.com, 11am-7pm Tues.-Sat., 11am-5pm Sun.), for instance, lures both residents and tourists with its clinical skin care ($55-140 pp), exotic spa treatments ($25-300 pp), and massage therapy ($50-160 pp). Specialties include the Thai yoga massage and the Prana Decadence, a complete three-hour experience that includes a body polishing scrub, a 75-minute body massage, an ultimate foot treatment, a 60-minute ultimate rejuvenation facial, and a shirodhara warm oil hair and scalp treatment.

White Street Healing Arts (1217 White St., 305/393-4102, 305/296-5997, or 305/304-5891, www.whitestreethealingarts.com, by appointment) is a holistic professional group that provides massage therapy in addition to acupuncture, chiropractic and Chinese medicine, and intuitive healing. Offerings include Swedish, deep tissue, aromatherapy, and reflexology massage ($90 hourly, $110 per 75 minutes, $130 per 90 minutes), plus hot stone massage ($165 per 90 minutes) and couples massage ($180 hourly, $220 per 75 minutes, $260 per 90 minutes). The licensed massage therapists here are often willing to bring their skills directly to you, but a 24-hour cancellation policy is in effect for all appointments, whether inside or outside the office.

In New Town, on the eastern part of the island, the **All About You Day Spa & Wellness Centre** (1712-1714 N. Roosevelt Blvd., 305/292-0818, www.allaboutyoukw.com, by appointment Mon., 7am-6pm Tues.-Sat.) features an assortment of salon and spa services, including perms, glycolic peels, waxing, and permanent make-up. As at other Key West day spas, you can opt for manicures ($20-35 pp), pedicures ($30-65 pp), facials ($45-100 pp), body wraps ($75-150 pp), and massage treatments ($50-140 pp). Two favorites are the 90-minute hot rock massage and the 60-minute monkeybar massage, during which a licensed massage therapist uses suspended parallel bars to perform a tabletop Shiatsu massage. Farther east, the **Solar Spa of Key West** (2824 N. Roosevelt Blvd., 305/292-6080, www.solarspaofkeywest.com, 10am-7pm Mon.-Sat.), a day spa and tanning salon, offers standard services, such as hair care (rates vary), manicures ($25 pp), pedicures ($35 pp), facials ($75 pp), body treatments ($120 pp), and massages ($80-100 pp).

For relaxation of a more active variety, consider **Yoga on the Beach** (305/296-7352, www.yogaonbeach.com), which offers daily, year-round classes on the beach, either at Fort Zachary Taylor Historic State Park or the Southernmost on the Beach property. Classes at the state park, which can range between the hour-long Yoga Express and the 90-minute Yoga for Every Body, typically cost $15 per person and include the park entrance fee. Meanwhile, classes at Southernmost on the Beach, such as the hour-long Yin Yoga, typically cost $10 for hotel guests and $15 for drop-in clients. Mats, blankets, and props are provided for all classes, and instructors will make every effort to accommodate those with disabilities.

Accommodations

Key West has, by far, the greatest assortment of lodging options in the Florida Keys, from intimate bed-and-breakfasts to sprawling resorts—only some of which are listed here. Organizations like the **Key West Innkeepers Association** (KWIA, 305/295-9500 or 800/492-1911, www.keywestinns.com) or **The Lodging Association of the Florida Keys and Key West** (3152 Northside Dr., Ste. 101, 305/296-4959, www.keyslodging.org) can help you choose the place that's right for you. No matter where you decide to stay, reservations are highly recommended, especially on weekends during the peak season (Dec.-Apr.).

$100-200

Conceived to honor the many literary masters who lived and worked in Key West, the **Authors Key West Guesthouse** (725 White St., 305/294-7381 or 800/898-6909, www.authorskeywest.com, $100-135 d) provides a compound of Conch-style houses, suites, and rooms. Typically named after famous writers or artists, the accommodations range from the John James Audubon room, which contains a queen-size bed and a private bath, to

the Ernest Hemingway cottage, which offers, in addition to a queen-size bed, a trundle bed, a living room, and a full kitchen. Whether you choose to swim in the heated pool or sip an evening cocktail in the garden, the Authors Guesthouse may be the perfect place to start that novel you've always wanted to write.

Nestled amid the varied lodgings on Fleming, the ecofriendly **Eden House** (1015 Fleming St., 305/296-6868 or 800/533-5397, www.edenhouse.com, $125-330 d) offers the ideal setting for a wide variety of visitors, from couples on a romantic getaway to large family reunions. Composed of an art deco-style main building and several renovated Conch-style houses, the Eden House seems a world away from Duval Street, though it lies within walking distance of the busy thoroughfare. While not technically a spa resort, this picturesque place—which once served as the backdrop for *CrissCross,* a film starring Goldie Hawn—certainly has the ambience of one. Surrounded by the lovely buildings, the main focus of the complex is the freshwater pool area, where you'll find shady palm trees, gurgling fountains, numerous tables and chairs, a peaceful gazebo, a sun deck, and a six-person hot tub. Although the rooms and suites vary in size and amenities—from a cozy spot beside the pool to a two-level house with a hot tub of its own—all guests can enjoy the hotel's varied features, including a comfortable library area, relaxing hammocks, wireless Internet access, beach towels that can be used off-site, a daily happy hour beside the pool, a 24-hour staff, and complimentary coffee and tea in the lobby. As a bonus, the Eden House will let you store your luggage even after you check out, so that you can savor a few more hours in Key West.

The motto at the **Garden House Bed & Breakfast** (329 Elizabeth St., 305/296-5368 or 800/695-6453, www.key-west-florida-bed-breakfast.com, $159-219 d) encourages guests to "leave the grumpy attitude at home." That's pretty easy to do when you spot the sumptuous grounds, which include an upper-level sun deck as well as a heated pool with spa jets and a cascading waterfall, all surrounded by lush

tropical gardens. There are 10 uniquely decorated rooms on-site—ranging from the Gecko Grotto, with its queen-size bed and private bath, to the Writer's King, with its Tiffany-style reading lamps and king-size bed. Not far away, in a quiet area of Old Town, the **Rose Lane Villas** (522-524 Rose Ln., 305/292-2170, www.roselanevillas.com, one-bedroom villas $159-269 d, two-bedroom and three-bedroom villas $402-666) provide a tempting haven for those who want to stay within walking distance of the action. Though the one-bedroom, two-bedroom, and three-bedroom villas vary in size, each has a full kitchen, cable television, free wireless Internet access, and an allotted parking space. Before hitting the town, take an early morning swim in the beautiful pool, accented by a stunning mural of lush gardens. After a long day exploring Key West, finish your evening with a cocktail on one of the peaceful porches or balconies and listen to the murmur of Old Town fading into the night.

Between the grand two-story Victorian mansion and the poolside cabana, the **Pilot House Guest House** (414 Simonton St., 305/293-6600 or 800/648-3780, www.pilothousekey-west.com, $130-210 d) encompasses a variety of accommodations to suit every traveler's needs, ranging from a standard room with a private bathroom, a kitchenette, a queen-size bed, and a balcony to the King Cabana II, which contains a king-size bed, a kitchenette, a Jacuzzi tub, and a private bathroom with a European shower. The grounds also feature a beautiful pool and a semi-private spa, both of which are clothing-optional. The **Mango Tree Inn** (603 Southard St., 305/293-1177, www.mangotree-inn.com, $129-189 d), constructed in 1858, is a gorgeous example of Old Town's historical architecture. Inside, the inn offers comfortable rooms, some with two bedrooms and full kitchens. Relax with a swim in the pool, surrounded by lush gardens and tall palm trees, or chat with the resident celebrities: Jade the parrot and Leilani the cockatoo.

Just two blocks off Duval, **The Paradise Inn** (819 Simonton St., 305/293-8007 or 800/888-9648, www.theparadiseinn.com, $169-199 d)

Eden House features a palm-shaded oasis, surrounded by several different historic structures.

© LAURA MARTONE

provides elegant suites, ranging from a mini suite with two queen-size beds to the Royal Poinciana Suite, featuring two bedrooms, two bathrooms with Jacuzzi tubs, and a wrap-around porch. The grounds, teeming with tropical flora, include a Jacuzzi and a fountain-fed pool. What was once, in the 1920s, a bor-dello and gambling spot has become a simple and affordable place to stay in Key West. At the **Angelina Guest House** (302 Angela St., 305/294-4480 or 888/303-4480, www.angelinaguesthouse.com, $104-149 d), "simple" means having no phones or televisions, allow-ing you to truly escape your daily existence. Only two blocks from the hustle and bustle of Duval, you'll find infinite tranquility in the verdant garden and heated lagoon-style pool. Here the accommodations vary from having a shared bathroom and full-size beds to hav-ing a king-size bed, a private bathroom, and a refrigerator.

The **Truman Hotel** (611 Truman Ave., 305/296-6700 or 866/487-8626, www.tru-manhotel.com, $169-199 d), one of the newer boutique hotels in town, prides itself on being "South Beach hip with a Key West flair." With accommodations that range from a standard room to a suite featuring two king-size beds and a living room, each selection contains swanky touches like zebra-striped rugs, leather chairs, and modern lighting. As a bonus, after a long day wandering around Key West, you'll relish a dip in the combination pool and spa.

Among the more reasonable offerings in the Old Town section of Key West is the histori-cal ⓒ **Chelsea House Pool and Gardens** (709 Truman Ave., 800/845-8859, www.historick-eywestinns.com, $170-220 d), which consists of two grand Victorian mansions on an acre of lush tropical gardens. Dating from 1888 and 1906, these two former homes now contain a variety of comfortable guest rooms and suites, with amenities like private bathrooms, cable television, and air-conditioning. Other features include a continental breakfast, a heated pool, on-site parking, free wireless Internet access in the courtyard, and proximity to Key West's most popular restaurants and attractions. With

advance arrangements, you might also be able to bring your pet during your stay. After all, the Chelsea House was named for a cat (a British shorthair named Chelsea) that lived here in the 1970s.

The adults-only **Azul Key West** (907 Truman Ave., 305/296-5152, www.azulhotels. us, $159-219 d) features 11 rooms and suites surrounding a beautiful freshwater pool. Each room includes a king-size bed, a flat-screen tele-vision, and wireless Internet access. The suites, meanwhile, range from those possessing shared balconies, with views of the pool or Truman Avenue, to the Aria Suite, situated at treetop level and offering stunning views of the entire area. As an alternative, head toward the quieter end of Duval, where the **La Te Da Hotel** (1125 Duval St., 305/296-6706 or 877/528-3320, www.lateda.com, $100-200 d) features plenty of activities to distract you from the "Duval crawl." Two bars, a restaurant, and a cabaret only add to the charm of this beautiful hotel. The accommodations here range from standard rooms with two queen-size beds, a refrigerator, and cable television to luxury rooms featuring extra touches like British Colonial-style fur-nishings and 800-thread-count linens.

The **El Patio Motel** (800 Washington St., 305/296-6531 or 866/533-5189, www.elpa-tiomotel.com, $96-169 d), a 30-room motel designed in the art deco style, features a lush tropical garden, a serene fountain, and a fresh-water swimming pool. Accommodations here range from a basic room with a refrigerator to an apartment with a full kitchen. In addition, limited wireless Internet access is available, de-pending on your location on the property.

OVER $200

Given that it's also a respected museum, **The Curry Mansion Inn** (511 Caroline St., 305/294-5349 or 800/253-3466, www.currymansion. com, $195-240 d) is surprisingly accommodat-ing to its guests. The historical 22-room prop-erty contains various types of lodgings, from standard deluxe bedrooms with king-size beds and private bathrooms to magnificent master suites featuring large balconies, comfortable sitting rooms, and cable television. Situated within the bustling heart of Old Town, the Curry still allows you a modicum of peace and quiet, whether you're dining on a full breakfast, enjoying an afternoon cocktail party, swimming in the on-site pool, or simply relaxing on the grounds.

Northeast of the Curry, the **Cypress House** (601 Caroline St., 305/294-5229, www.cypresshousekw.com, $155-325 d) offers comfortable, bed-and-breakfast accommodations in a historical Conch-style building that was erected in 1888. Guests can expect spacious, high-ceilinged rooms with air-conditioning, ceiling fans, cable television, refrigerators, bathrobes, and complimentary, high-speed wireless Internet access. Other amenities on this locked, gated property include lush tropical gardens, a heated swimming pool, bicycle rentals, parking ($10 daily), a continental breakfast buffet (8am-11am daily), and complimentary cocktails (6pm-7pm daily). Note that minimum stay

© DANIEL MARTONE

the elegant Marquesa Hotel and Marquesa Cottages

requirements vary seasonally, and guests must be at least 16 years of age.

Two blocks south of the Cypress House, the white, casually elegant, Conch-style **Marquesa Hotel and Marquesa Cottages** (600 Fleming St., 305/292-1919, www.marquesa.com, $190-345 d), originally built in 1884, provide luxuriously furnished hotel rooms and private well-equipped cottages. All chambers are clean, comfortable, and airy, with tropical-style touches like wooden floors, ceiling fans, and vibrant paintings. Despite its proximity to Duval Street, the Marquesa still offers enough of a buffer to make it feel as though you've found a quiet little nook of your own. That's especially true in the well-landscaped pool and garden area, which features a waterfall, two freshwater pools, and numerous chaise lounges and shaded tables. Other property amenities include wireless Internet access and an upscale restaurant, open to hotel guests as well as the public. Farther south, **The Mermaid & The Alligator Bed & Breakfast** (729 Truman Ave., 305/294-1894 or 800/773-1894, www.kwmermaid.com, $148-318 d) truly aspires to be "your home in Key West." This beautiful 1904 Victorian-style home offers eight unique rooms in the main house in addition to a Conch-style cottage on the grounds. Amenities include a full complimentary breakfast, a lush garden, and a heated pool, featuring built-in benches and whirlpool jets.

The stylish **Santa Maria Suites** (1401 Simonton St., 305/296-5678 or 866/726-8259, www.santamariasuites.com, $249-279 d) feature accommodations with private balconies and terraces. Only a block from the Atlantic Ocean and not far from Duval, this lovely hotel provides an escape from the craziness of Key West. The accommodations vary from standard one-bedroom suites to luxury two-bedroom bi-level suites. Other amenities include flat-screen televisions and two heated, garden-enclosed swimming pools.

Closer to the ocean, the magnificent Spanish-style **Casa Marina Resort** (1500 Reynolds St., 305/296-3535 or 888/303-5717, www.casamarinaresort.com, $239-279 d) beckons an upscale clientele with its cream-colored walls, red roof tiles, and arched entryways. Built in 1920 and now part of the Waldorf Astoria Collection, the largest resort in Key West comprises a wide array of elegantly furnished rooms and suites, from the Island Vista, with two double beds, to the Ocean Vista two-bedroom suite, featuring 900 square feet of space. All accommodations include a mini refrigerator and wireless Internet access. This grand resort also encompasses two enormous pools, a beautiful 1,100-foot beach with hammocks strung between palm trees, the Sun-Sun Beach Bar & Grill, and the Spa al Mare, where you can opt for massages, facials, aromatherapy, or a yoga session. In addition, guests can enjoy live entertainment in the on-site Rambler Lounge and savor a delicious steak at the Strip House, located at the hotel's sister property, The Reach Resort.

Situated on seven waterfront acres on the eastern side of the island, the **Key West Marriott Beachside Hotel** (3841 N. Roosevelt Blvd., 305/296-8100 or 800/546-0885, www.beachsidekeywest.com, $179-349 d) features luxurious accommodations, a lush tropical garden, a waterfront swimming pool, a sandy tanning beach, complete spa services, and immediate access to the on-site Tavern N' Town Restaurant. In addition, all guests can enjoy complimentary high-speed Internet service and flat-panel LCD televisions with cable.

Located on the gulf side of the island, **◖The Westin Key West Resort & Marina** (245 Front St., 305/294-4000 or 866/837-4250, www.westinkeywestresort.com, $450-575 d) provides splendid accommodations just steps from Mallory Square and the Custom House. This spacious resort features 178 luxurious guest rooms and suites, all of which include specially designed beds and showers, complimentary wireless Internet access, cable television, air-conditioning, and 24-hour room service, among other amenities. Some rooms and suites include flat-screen televisions, vaulted ceilings, Jacuzzi tubs, balconies, patios, and terrific views of the ocean, pool, courtyard, or gardens. Five hundred yards off the coast, the Westin

also boasts the **Sunset Key Guest Cottages** (305/292-5300 or 888/837-4249, www.westinsunsetkeycottages.com, $740-3,010), a sophisticated seven-acre resort on Sunset Key, a 27-acre residential island, where cars are not permitted. Offering seclusion from the hustle and bustle of Key West, the Sunset Key Guest Cottages contain one, two, three, or four bedrooms and can only be reached by ferry. Whether you choose to stay in Key West or on Sunset Key, you'll have access to all the amenities that the Westin resort offers, including the on-site marina, various water sports, a 24-hour fitness room and massage studio, a heated, palm-shaded outdoor pool, and several dining options, such as Bistro 245 and Latitudes. In addition, the Westin's Sunset Deck is an ideal spot from which to watch a famous Key West sunset.

Also within walking distance of Mallory Square, the **◖ Ocean Key Resort & Spa** (0 Duval St., 800/328-9815, www.oceankey.com, $279-550 d) provides fantastic sunset views and easy access to the heart of Key West. The luxurious, tropical-style accommodations range from a 600-square-foot junior suite with a king-size bed, a spacious living room, plasma television, and a private balcony, to a two-bedroom, 1,200-square-foot suite that's purportedly the largest suite on the island. On-site amenities include a heated outdoor pool, water-sports rentals, sailing and fishing trips arranged through the marina, unbelievable body treatments at SpaTerre, and the waterfront Hot Tin Roof restaurant. Situated across the street, the **Pier House Resort and Caribbean Spa** (1 Duval St., 305/296-4600 or 800/723-2791, www.pierhouse.com, $299-575 d) has been serving guests since 1979. Known as the first true resort on the island, Pier House encompasses a private beach, a heated outdoor pool, and a private dock for charter pickups. While here, relax with a massage at the resort's world-class spa, savor a meal at the HarbourView Cafe or the Beach Bar and Grille, or consider deals like the Spa Honeymoon Package, which includes breakfast and a trip to the spa.

You'll be hard-pressed to miss the **Southernmost Hotel Collection**

(305/296-6577 or 800/354-4455, www.south-ernmostresorts.com, $300-659 d), set within Duval, United, and Simonton Streets. Each of the four hotels here offers sophisticated accommodations, sometimes with stunning ocean views: the airy 127-room **Southernmost Hotel** (1319 Duval St.), the tropical 123-room **Southernmost on the Beach** (508 South St.), and the elegant side-by-side Victorian-style boutique hotels, the 11-room **La Mer Hotel** and the eight-room **Dewey House** (508 South St.). No matter which property you choose, you'll be able to relax on the private beach, enjoy a dip in one of three pools, work out in the on-site fitness center, relish a delicious meal at the Southernmost Beach Café, sip cocktails at the Southernmost Tiki Bar, or of course, venture onto nearby Duval. Other amenities include free parking, lush gardens, and complimentary wireless Internet access.

Situated near the quieter end of Duval and built as a private residence in 1896, the colorful, Victorian-style ◖ **Southernmost House** (1400 Duval St., 305/296-3141, www.

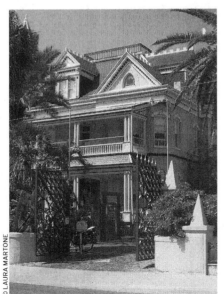

© LAURA MARTONE

the Victorian-style Southernmost House

southernmosthouse.com, $280-385 d) has seen its share of dignitaries, from Presidents Truman, Nixon, Kennedy, Eisenhower, and Carter to Key West fixtures like Ernest Hemingway. The accommodations here vary from the Southernmost Point Room, with its private balcony overlooking the Atlantic Ocean, to the Royal Suite, one of Key West's most favored suites, featuring a separate sitting parlor, stunning ocean and island views, and a four-poster king-size bed. While staying at the Southernmost House, refresh with a dip in the oceanside heated pool, then relax with a drink at the poolside bar.

The Reach Resort (1435 Simonton St., 305/296-5000 or 888/318-4316, www.reachresort.com, $319-419 d), part of the Waldorf Astoria Collection, is essentially a tropical playground. This boutique hotel provides the same experience you might receive from a Caribbean resort, with access to a spacious private beach; a variety of sailboats and water-sports gear; and a terrific spa (at its sister property, the Casa Marina Resort) to help renew your focus. Finish your evening with an exquisite meal at the on-site Strip House Steakhouse, before retiring to your luxury room or suite.

On the Atlantic Ocean, the **Coconut Beach Resort** (1500 Alberta St., 305/294-0057 or 800/835-0055, www.coconutbeachresort.com, studios $200-315 d, suites $310-550) contains a variety of accommodations, from studios to two-bedroom suites. In addition, the property features an open-deck pool and Jacuzzi, plus a small sandy beach. Farther inland, the adults-only **Olivia by Duval** (511 Olivia St., 305/296-5169 or 800/413-1978, www.oldtownsuites.com, $129-500 d) offers uniquely decorated rooms and suites, some of which include kitchenettes. Operated by Old Town Suites, this charming inn provides the perfect location for those hoping to experience the action of Duval while still enjoying the serenity of a private guesthouse. Amenities include cable television, air-conditioning, and a clothing-optional pool. For even more solitude, Old Town Suites also operates two lovely cottages on Center and Petronia Streets.

GAY AND LESBIAN LODGING

Key West is definitely a gay-friendly destination, as evidenced by Old Town's numerous gay bars and the city's annual events, from Pridefest to the ultimate bacchanal, Fantasy Fest. There are even several inns and resorts that cater to a gay and/or lesbian clientele.

The 38-room **Island House** (1129 Fleming St., 305/294-6284 or 800/890-6284, www.islandhousekeywest.com, $99-449 d), for instance, is Key West's largest gay male resort—and as some visitors have claimed, the classiest, most outrageous such place in the world. Within this secure, clothing-optional compound, gay men can relax and be themselves in an accepting environment, where a friendly all-male staff is available day and night. Here you'll find a swimming pool, a health club, a poolside bar and café, and a spa that includes a sauna, a five-man shower, and a Jacuzzi. The accommodations, meanwhile, are enclosed within four separate buildings, which were formerly a private residence, a boarding house, a Laundromat, and a cigar factory. The uniquely furnished lodgings range in size, though all have comfortable beds, extra-large bath towels, air-conditioning, and cable television.

In the same block, **Alexander's Guesthouse** (1118 Fleming St., 800/654-9919, www.alexanderskeywest.com, $145-290 d) welcomes a gay and lesbian clientele to a tranquil, comfortable setting, surrounded by lush tropical gardens. While here, you're free to enjoy the relaxing spa and sumptuous pool, which serves as the property's social center. Three levels of sun decks also allow guests a semiprivate setting to catch some rays and forget daily cares. Evenings at Alexander's begin with poolside cocktails, while in the morning, guests are greeted by a continental breakfast. No matter how you spend the time in between, however, you'll be sure to find a room that's right for you, as the inn houses a wide selection of airy accommodations, all individually decorated. In all, you'll find 15 comfortable guest rooms, one well-lit suite ($205-305 d) with a private patio, and a gorgeous apartment ($275-410) with wooden floors, a full kitchen, a private sun deck, and a front porch with a hammock.

Sixteen elegantly decorated guest rooms and suites make up the men-only **Coconut Grove** (815 Fleming St., 305/296-5107 or 800/262-6055, www.coconutgrovekeywest.com, $139-299 d), set within, as the name indicates, a lovely coconut grove. Featuring a secluded, heated pool and outdoor Jacuzzi, the inn serves wine and hors d'oeuvres nightly and a complimentary continental breakfast every morning. The accommodations range from a standard deluxe room to a presidential suite with two bedrooms, and all guests are welcome to use the free wireless Internet access.

Given that the Big Easy and the Southernmost City share so many common elements, it seems only fitting that you'd find the **New Orleans House** (724 Duval St., 305/293-9800 or 888/293-9893, www.neworleanshousekw.com, rooms and suites $110-220 d, cottages $175-390) in Key West's Old Town. As the new gay, all-male guesthouse on Duval, the New Orleans House puts you just steps away from all the action, including the on-site Bourbon St. Pub. Still, if you're looking to relax, you can do just that on the private sun deck overlooking the pool and hot tub. The accommodations here range from standard rooms with a shared bathroom to an intimate cottage, equipped with a full kitchen and a king-size bed. In all, you'll find eight rooms, one suite, and three cottages here.

Closer to the ocean lies one of the world's largest inns for women, including lesbians and gay-friendly heterosexuals. Just two blocks away from the southernmost point in the continental United States, **◖ Pearl's Rainbow** (525 United St., 305/292-1450 or 800/749-6696, www.pearlsrainbow.com, rooms $89-269 d, suites $199-379 d) offers a wide variety of 38 rooms and suites, ranging from the Skyview Room, with an angled ceiling and a queen-size bed, to the Deluxe Poolside Suite, equipped with a king-size bed, a poolside porch, and a living room with hand-painted furniture, a sofa bed, and two televisions. The property includes five separate structures—the Marrero Building, the Surf Building, the Louisa Cottage, the East Cottage, and the West Cottage—plus a parking lot, two freshwater pools, and two rejuvenating spas. Pearl's also features free wireless Internet access, a restaurant, and Key West's only tropical bar just for women. For more gay-friendly establishments, consult the **Key West Business Guild** (513 Truman Ave., 305/294-4603 or 800/535-7797, www.gaykeywestfl.com).

CAMPING

Although most people visiting Key West choose to stay in one of the city's varied inns, hotels, or resorts, campers will also find a few options on nearby Stock Island. South of the Key West Golf Club, **Boyd's Key West Campground** (6401 Maloney Ave., Stock Island, 305/294-1465, www.boydscampground.com, $55-120 daily) offers tent sites as well as RV spaces, many of which are equipped with water service, 30/50-amp electricity, sewer access, and cable television. Both inland and waterfront spots are available. In addition, the property features a heated swimming pool, a lounging beach, free wireless Internet access, and numerous planned activities, including craft and yoga classes, pot luck dinners, movie nights, line dancing, and casino cruises.

The intimate **El Mar RV Resort** (6700 Maloney Ave., Stock Island, 305/294-0857, www.elmarrvresort.com, $80-115 daily) caters to RV enthusiasts only. No tents, pop-ups, or truck campers are allowed. Situated on the ocean, the property offers 10 spaces in all, half of which have waterfront views. All of the lengthy gravel sites in this park feature patios and full hookups, including 30/50-amp electricity. Closer to the Overseas Highway and not far from the Hurricane Hole Marina, the family-operated **Leo's Campground** (5236 Suncrest Rd., Stock Island, 305/296-5260, www.leoscampground.com, $39-69 daily) welcomes tent and RV campers alike. Pets, however, are only allowed in the RV portion of the park, at a daily fee of $1 per pet. There are also charges for extra people ($8 daily) and trailers ($7 daily). The tent sites, most of which have barbecue grills and picnic tables, are situated along a small, quiet lake, surrounded by mangroves, while the RV spaces feature picnic tables, 70-channel cable television, and full hookups with 30/50-amp electricity. Other on-site amenities include a barbecue area for RV campers, a laundry facility, and a bathhouse with hot showers. Monthly rates ($990-1,550) are also available.

Food

As with lodging options, Key West has the largest selection of restaurants in the Florida Keys, and the cuisine down here runs the gamut from fresh seafood to all-American hamburgers to upscale French and Italian dishes. So whatever your mood, you're sure to find something tasty in the Southernmost City. Of course, only a small percentage of the available eateries are listed here. For more suggestions, consult the **Florida Keys Dining Guide** (www.keysdining.com).

SEAFOOD

Key West, like the rest of the Florida Keys, boasts a plethora of fresh seafood options,

especially near the Historic Seaport at Key West Bight. While meandering around this lively area, be sure to stop by the **Half Shell Raw Bar** (231 Margaret St., 305/294-7496, www.halfshellrawbar.com, 11am-10pm daily, $7-21), a former shrimp-packing facility that has maintained its charm as an authentic fish house. Though offering fried dishes, this laid-back eatery really specializes in raw, steamed, broiled, and grilled seafood. After starting with a bucket of steamed clams, try the stuffed shrimp, prepared with crabmeat and spices and broiled with garlic butter, white wine, and lemon juice.

Along the boardwalk, you can enjoy fresh seafood on the breezy upper deck of the weathered 🄲 **Schooner Wharf Bar** (202 William St., 305/292-3302, www.schoonerwharf.com, 7:30am-4am daily, $8-18). Here you'll find standard Keys fare like the filling seafood sampler, featuring conch fritters, mahimahi, four kinds of shrimp, and fries. In addition, the Schooner Wharf now serves complete breakfasts, such as the shrimp Benedict Florentine. This casual, open-air watering hole also offers live music, starting at noon and continuing late into the night.

Also beside the harbor, the **Conch Republic Seafood Company** (631 Greene St., 305/294-4403, www.conchrepublicseafood.com, 11am-midnight daily, $8-28) provides a casual atmosphere for seafood lovers. Here you'll enjoy raw oysters and clams, traditional dishes like grilled dolphin (mahimahi), 80 different varieties of rum, and daily entertainment, with musicians often playing late into the evening.

Within the **A&B Lobster House** (700 Front St., 305/294-5880, www.aandblobsterhouse. com, 6pm-11pm daily, $24-70), a fancy, white-cloth restaurant that offers signature dishes like grouper Oscar and tuna au poivre, you'll find **Alonzo's Oyster Bar** (www.alonzosoysterbar. com, 11am-10pm Mon.-Sat., noon-10pm Sun., $9-28), a casual eatery that serves key lime garlic oysters, steamed shrimp, roasted mussels, and other tasty treats.

Though not as old or as legendary as some Key West eateries, the family-owned **Two Friends Patio Restaurant** (512 Front St., 305/296-3124, www.twofriendskeywest.com, 8am-close daily, $9-35) is still a lively choice for breakfast, lunch, and dinner. Established in 1967, this open-air eatery prepares filling breakfast dishes like shrimp and crabmeat quiche and crab cake Benedict, as well as terrific "chargrilled" steaks, fresh seafood dishes, and tropical drinks later in the day. As a bonus, you'll find early-bird specials from 4 to 7pm daily, plus live karaoke nightly. Even if you never work up the nerve to take the stage, you'll certainly enjoy the show, and if you're a seafood fan, you can't go wrong at a place

© LAURA MARTONE

Tourists flock to the Two Friends Patio Restaurant.

Several eateries lie near the Historic Seaport, including the Turtle Kraals Restaurant & Bar.

that offers everything from conch fritters and raw oysters to a lobster combo platter that includes grilled gulf shrimp, broiled scallops, and a whole Florida lobster tail.

Closer to the ocean, you'll spot **Pisces** (1007 Simonton St., 305/294-7100, www.pisceskeywest.com, 6pm-11pm daily, $23-44), another fine-dining seafood establishment. Here you can enjoy a taste of New Orleans with the grilled shrimp Nola, or try the black grouper bouillabaisse with mussels, clams, and calamari. Other favorites include Lobster Tango Mango and Yellowtail Snapper Atocha. Pisces is the ideal place for a candlelit dinner, which might explain why reservations are recommended year-round. For an alternative experience, head to the **Hurricane Hole Restaurant & Marina** (5130 Overseas Hwy., Stock Island, 305/294-0200, www.hurricaneholekeywest. com, 11am-10pm daily, $11-23), where you can enjoy fresh seafood, steak, and chicken, while overlooking the marina. Bring in some freshly caught fish, and the cooks will grill, blacken, or fry it for you.

AMERICAN AND VEGETARIAN

Seafood isn't the only option for gourmands in Key West. Burgers, steaks, barbecue, even vegetarian dishes are available, too. If you're looking for a well-prepared steak, head first to the **Prime Steakhouse** (951 Caroline St., 305/296-4000, www.primekeywest.com, 6pm-10:30pm daily, $22-48), a fine-dining steakhouse that also offers an excellent selection of complementary wines. Begin with a signature martini before sampling one of the steak specials. Reservations are recommended, especially during the high season. The newly remodeled **Turtle Kraals Restaurant & Bar** (231 Margaret St., 305/294-2640, www.turtlekraals.com, 7am-10pm daily, $8-22) serves typical Keys-style dishes for breakfast, lunch, and dinner, though it definitely specializes in barbecue. Both the quaint indoor dining area and the covered outdoor patio provide the ideal atmosphere for enjoying a barbecue beef brisket platter or one of several other choice selections.

Just a few steps from Duval Street, lies the **Island Dogs Bar** (505 Front St., 305/509-7136, www.islanddogsbar.com, 11am-4am daily, $8-15), one of the few late-night joints in town. So when most restaurants are closed, head directly to this casual bar and eatery, which serves food until 3:30am every night. Here you'll find all-American favorites like chicken wings, hot dogs, burgers, and sandwiches, not to mention an array of alcoholic libations. Both indoor and outdoor seating are available.

C Sloppy Joe's Bar (201 Duval St., 305/294-5717, www.sloppyjoes.com, 9am-close daily, $4-13)—a spacious, boxy, white building that's hard to miss with its red-brick columns and the bar's name in giant, black letters—has been a Key West tradition since 1933. Supposedly one of Ernest Hemingway's favorite Key West watering holes, Sloppy Joe's has run an annual Hemingway Look-Alike Contest since 1980. The menu is fairly extensive, with traditional Key West-style cuisine as well as the famous Original Sloppy Joe Sandwich, which features delicious ground beef in a rich tomato sauce with onions, peppers, and spices. The food isn't the only attraction here; various bands keep you entertained day and night.

If you enjoy listening to good music while noshing on good food, then you're in luck. Sloppy Joe's isn't the only game in town. **Willie T's Restaurant & Bar** (525 Duval St., 305/294-7674, www.williets.com, 11am-2am daily, $11-17) also offers live music, excellent food, and terrific libations. In fact, the menu includes 28 different mojitos, from key lime to ginger to espresso. As for the food, Willie T's provides an assortment of tasty dishes, from the goat cheese and avocado salad to the blackened dolphin with avocado butter and red pepper jam.

For an organic, vegetarian meal, stroll over to **Help Yourself** (829 Fleming St., 305/296-7766, www.helpyourselffoods.com, 8am-7pm Mon.-Sat., 8am-3pm Sun., $8-14), which features a fairly extensive menu, including lasagna made with layers of zucchini, brazil nut meat, spinach, pesto, fresh tomatoes, and marinara. If you're just looking for a quick snack, consider ordering a refreshing smoothie, such as the Chocolate Buzz, made with cacao powder, cacao nibs, and banana.

For a variety of options, stroll toward Key West Bight, where **The Commodore Waterfront Restaurant** (700 Front St., 305/294-9191, www.commodorekeywest.com, 5:30pm-10:30pm daily, $20-38) features traditional Florida Keys-style dishes, including seafood and steaks, in a fine-dining setting along the waterfront. Farther inland, you'll encounter another winning option, **Kelly's Caribbean Bar, Grill & Brewery** (301 Whitehead St., 305/293-8484, www.kellyscaribbean.blogspot.com, 11am-11pm daily, $16-30). Known as the birthplace of Pan American Airlines and now home to the Southernmost Brewery, Kelly's presents a menu of island flavors with such tasty dishes as coconut shrimp and jerked chicken. The food is delicious, but the real draw is the beer, crafted by the on-site brewmaster. Be sure to try Kelly's flagship beer, the Havana Red Ale.

Only a block off Duval, the classy, often noisy, **C Café Marquesa** (600 Fleming St., 305/292-1244, www.marquesa.com, 6pm-10pm daily, $20-49) feels as though it could be in Manhattan. The 50-seat restaurant offers contemporary American cuisine like macadamia-crusted yellowtail or pan-roasted duck breast. Whether you're a guest of the adjacent Marquesa Hotel or you're just looking for a fantastic place to start the evening, this small hot spot provides an elegant alternative to Key West's casual waterfront eateries.

The **Blue Heaven Restaurant** (729 Thomas St., 305/296-8666, www.blueheavenkw.com, 8am-close, $7-20) has been serving breakfast, lunch, and dinner since 1992. The full menu features everything from pancakes to Caribbean barbecue shrimp. For dessert, try the Banana Heaven, a banana bread with bananas flambéed in rum, served with vanilla ice cream.

Headed toward the ocean side of Old Town, you'll spot **Camille's Restaurant** (1202 Simonton St., 305/296-4811, www.camilleskeywest.com, 8am-3pm and 6pm-10pm daily, $6-28), a fun, exotic eatery that features fondue to veal saltimbocca, featuring sautéed veal, topped with prosciutto di parma, yellow tomatoes, fresh sage, manchego cheese, and a velvety cream sauce. As a bonus, from 5:30 to 7:30pm, Michaels serves a new light-side menu, featuring smaller versions of all available dishes.

On Duval, you'll spot  **Martin's Restaurant & Lounge** (917 Duval St., 305/295-0111, www.martinskeywest.com, 5:30pm-11pm daily, $23-49), a stylish German fusion restaurant that offers scrumptious dinner options as well as a terrific weekend brunch, featuring specialties like grilled bratwurst, seafood crepes, and eggs Benedict with lobster medallions. Both the menu and the decor illustrate a superb blend of classical and tropical attributes, with a touch of European sophistication. The space is divided into three unique sections: the elegant dining room, the chic lounge, and the sumptuous garden. Unlike many fine restaurants, Martin's welcomes children, which means that busy parents can enjoy delicious food, but couples without kids may find a quiet, romantic meal less than probable.

Café Marquesa, an upscale restaurant adjacent to the Marquesa Hotel

Photo credit (vertical): © DANIEL MARTONE

breakfast, lunch, and dinner. Unique dishes include a three-egg omelet made with fresh lobster, or the tender veal with an Asian panko crust. Despite the delicious food, though, the prevalent sexual innuendos in Camille's might not make it the most family-friendly establishment in town. As an alternative, stroll over to the **Flaming Buoy Filet Co.** (1100 Packer St., 305/295-7970, www.theflamingbuoy.com, 6pm-9:30pm daily, $18-48), where you can savor a New York strip steak with blue cheese butter, or the mojito chicken with fried plantains and brown rice. If you'd prefer to stay in your hotel, take advantage of the Flaming Buoy's delivery option.

EUROPEAN

Situated in a garden oasis,  **Michaels Restaurant** (532 Margaret St., 305/295-1300, www.michaelskeywest.com, 5:30pm-10pm daily, $7-19) provides one of the most romantic dining opportunities in Key West. The menu features a variety of dishes, from

FRENCH

While you won't find too many options for French cuisine in the Southernmost City, there are definitely two standouts. The **Banana Cafe** (1215 Duval St., 305/294-7227, www.bananacafekw.com, 8am-3pm daily, 6pm-10pm Tues.-Sat., $7-30), for instance, is a popular French-style eatery that specializes in delectable crepes for breakfast, including the tasty La Ratatouille, which features cooked eggplant, zucchini, onions, tomatoes, and varied peppers, wrapped in a crepe and topped with a fried egg. The dinner menu is also divine, offering such winners as mussels Brittany or a Parisian-style ribeye. Popular with couples in a romantic mood, **Café Solé** (1029 Southard St., 305/294-0230, www.cafesole.com, 5:30pm-10pm daily, $18-23) combines French sauces with locally caught seafood. Fish dominates the menu, which includes such favorites as grouper Romesco, served with garlic, tomatoes, and a spicy roasted red pepper and hazelnut sauce,

scrumptious Peanut Butter Perversion at Better Than Sex

and tuna seared in pistachios with wasabi cream and a hoisin garlic sauce.

MEDITERRANEAN

For authentic Italian cuisine, look no farther than **Mangia Mangia Pasta Cafe** (900 Southard St., 305/294-2469, www.mangiamangia.com, 5:30pm-10pm daily, $10-28). Situated in the heart of Old Town, this corner restaurant channels the ambience of a small Italian village. Here you'll find an array of fresh pastas with delicious homemade sauces, such as the New Zealand mussels with spaghettini, prepared in a garlic-based marinara sauce and topped with shaved parmesan cheese.

If you have a craving for various Mediterranean flavors, visit the well-regarded **Azur Restaurant** (425 Grinnell St., 305/292-2987, www.azurkeywest.com, 8am-2pm and 6pm-10pm Mon.-Fri., 9am-2pm and 6pm-10pm Sat., 10am-2pm Sun., $6-36) beside the Eden House. Serving breakfast, lunch, and dinner on the shaded terrace or in the dining room, Azur features such delicious creations as Brie and mushroom omelets; charred octopus marinated with garlic, lemon zest, and Italian parsley; and apple and almond tarts with cardamom ice cream.

DESSERT

If you're a dessert connoisseur, you'll definitely find a lot of key lime pie in the eateries of Key West, but that's not the only treat that the Southernmost City has to offer. For something cool on a warm afternoon, head to the **Key West Ice Cream Factory** (201 William St., 305/295-3011, www.keywesticecreamfactory.com, 11am-10pm daily, $7-19). Offering 33 flavors of ice cream, including "Conchy" Cookies 'N Cream or Bermuda Triangle Chocolate, the shop also features 15 flavors of sorbet, including cantaloupe and watermelon. Just be prepared for long waits. Later in the evening, you should skip dinner altogether and head directly to **Better Than Sex** (926 Simonton St., 305/296-8102, www.betterthansexkw.com, 6pm-1am Tues.-Sun. Christmas-Easter, 6pm-1am Wed.-Sun.

Apr.-Dec., $9-13), a bordello-style lounge that prepares unforgettable desserts, such as Peanut Butter Perversion, the Missionary Crisp, and Kinky Key Lime, a creamy mousse concoction that just might be the best key lime pie in town. Enhance your visit to this exotic, infinitely romantic spot with a glass of dark chocolate-rimmed Merlot.

Information and Services

INFORMATION
Tourism and Government Offices

For brochures, maps, and other information about Key West, plus assistance with hotel and tour reservations, stop by the **Key West Visitors Center** (1601 N. Roosevelt Blvd., 305/296-8881 or 877/296-8881, www.keywest123.com, 8am-10pm daily), the **Key West Chamber of Commerce** (510 Greene St., 1st Fl., 305/294-2587, www.keywestchamber.org, 8am-6:30pm daily), or the **Key West Information Center** (201 Front St., Ste. 108, 888/222-5590, www.keywestinfo.com, 9am-5pm Mon.-Sat.). In addition, you can consult the **Key West Attractions Association (KWAA)** (www.keywestattractions.org), **Key West's Finest** (1107 Key Plaza, Ste. 310, 305/296-0555, www.keywestfinest.com), or the **Monroe County Tourist Development Council** (1201 White St., Ste. 102, 305/296-1552 or 800/352-5397, www.fla-keys.com, 9am-5pm Mon.-Fri.). You can even save money on sightseeing adventures through online companies like **Trusted Tours and Attractions** (800/844-7601, www.trustedtours.com).

For government-related issues, contact the **City of Key West** (525 Angela St., 305/809-3700, www.keywestcity.com, 8am-5pm Mon.-Fri.) or the **Monroe County offices** (1100 Simonton St., 305/294-4641, www.monroecounty-fl.gov, 8am-5pm Mon.-Fri.).

Media

For local news, consult the daily *The Key West Citizen* (www.keysnews.com), the *Key West Keynoter* (www.keysnet.com), or *The Weekly Newspapers* (www.keysweekly.com). The daily *Miami Herald* (www.miamiherald.com) and the biweekly *Florida Keys Keynoter* (www.keysnet.com) are also available throughout the Keys.

In Key West, you'll also have access to several radio stations, including the popular **US-1 Radio** (104.1 FM, http://us1radio.com), which offers local news, including up-to-the-minute weather information during hurricane season. In addition, most hotels offer access to the major television stations in the Miami-Fort Lauderdale market.

SERVICES
Money

For banking needs, stop by **Capital Bank** (330 Whitehead St., 305/294-6330 or 800/639-5111, www.capitalbank-us.com, 9am-4pm Mon.-Thurs., 9am-6pm Fri., extended drive-through hours). Another option is the **First State Bank of the Florida Keys** (www.keysbank.com), which offers five locations in the Key West area, from Stock Island (5450 MacDonald Ave., 305/296-8535, 9am-4pm Mon.-Thurs., 9am-6pm Fri., extended drive-through hours) to Old Town (444 Whitehead St., 305/296-8535, 9am-4pm Mon.-Thurs., 9am-6pm Fri.).

Mail

For shipping, faxing, copying, and other business-related services, visit **The UPS Store** (2900 N. Roosevelt Blvd., Ste. 1107, 305/292-4177, www.theupsstore.com, 9am-6pm Mon.-Fri., 10am-3pm Sat.). You can also package and ship items at the two local **post offices** (800/275-8777, www.usps.com). You'll find one on the eastern end of the island (2764 N. Roosevelt Blvd., 305/296-7327, 8:30am-5pm Mon.-Fri.,

9am-noon Sat.) and one in Old Town (400 Whitehead St., 305/294-9539, 8:30am-5pm Mon.-Fri., 9:30am-noon Sat.).

Groceries and Supplies

For groceries, baked goods, and other supplies, head to the nearest **Winn-Dixie** (2778 N. Roosevelt Blvd., 305/294-0491, www.winndixie.com, 24 hours daily), which has an on-site pharmacy (305/294-0658, 8am-8pm Mon.-Fri., 9am-7pm Sat.-Sun.). In Key West, you'll also find a **Publix** (3316 N. Roosevelt Blvd., 305/296-2225, www.publix.com, 7am-10pm Mon.-Sat., 7am-9pm Sun.), which includes an on-site pharmacy (305/296-3225, 9am-9pm Mon.-Fri., 9am-7pm Sat., 10am-5pm Sun.). The area also features a **CVS/pharmacy** (530 Truman Ave., 305/294-2576, www.cvs.com, 24 hours daily), which offers limited supplies as well as an on-site pharmacy (9am-9pm Mon.-Sat., 10am-6pm Sun.).

Laundry

If you need to clean some clothes during your trip, you'll find several coin-operated laundries in the area, including two locations of **Key West Laundries** (www.keywestlaundry.com): the **Key West Launderette** (912 Kennedy Dr., 7am-10pm daily) and the **Habana Plaza Coin Laundry** (3124 Flagler Ave., 7am-10pm daily).

Internet Access

Using your own laptop, you can access high-speed wireless Internet service at any number of hotels and resorts in the Key West area. In addition, there are several charming Internet cafés, including the **Coffee Plantation** (713 Caroline St., 305/295-9808, www.coffeeplantationkeywest.com, 7am-6pm daily) and the **Sippin' Internet Cafe** (424 Eaton St., 305/293-0555, www.sippinkeywest.com, 7am-11pm daily). You'll also find useful services, including Internet access, at the **Monroe County May Hill Russell Library** (700 Fleming St., 305/292-3595, www.keyslibraries.org, 9:30am-6pm Tues. and Thurs.-Fri., 9:30am-8pm Wed., 10am-6pm Sat.).

Emergency Services

In case of an emergency that requires police, fire, or ambulance services, dial **911** from any cell or public phone. For nonemergency assistance, contact the **Monroe County Sheriff's Office** (5525 College Rd., 305/292-7000, www.keysso.net, 8am-5pm Mon.-Fri.). For medical assistance, consult the **Lower Keys Medical Center** (5900 College Rd., Stock Island, 305/294-5531, www.lkmc.com). Foreign visitors seeking help with directions, medical concerns, business issues, law enforcement needs, or other problems can receive **multilingual tourist assistance** (800/771-5397) 24 hours daily.

Getting There and Around

GETTING THERE
By Air

Travelers can reach Key West directly by flying into the **Key West International Airport (EYW)** (3491 S. Roosevelt Blvd., 305/809-5200 or 305/296-5439, www.keywestinternationalairport.com). Besides major airlines, such as **US Airways** (800/428-4322, www.usairways.com) and **Delta Air Lines** (800/221-1212, www.delta.com), the Key West airport hosts smaller air carriers, like **Cape Air** (508/771-6944 or 800/352-0714, www.capeair.com, rates vary), which offers daily service between Fort Myers and Key West.

Other area airports include the **Florida Keys Marathon Airport (MTH)** (9400 Overseas Hwy., Marathon, 305/289-6060), the **Fort Lauderdale-Hollywood International Airport (FLL)** (100 Terminal Dr., Fort Lauderdale, 866/435-9355, www.broward.org/airport), and the **Miami International Airport (MIA)** (2100 NW 42nd Ave., Miami, 305/876-7000 or 800/825-5642, www.miami-airport.com). From each airport, you can rent a vehicle from such agencies as **Avis** (800/331-1212, www. avis.com), **Budget** (800/527-0700, www.budget.com), **Enterprise** (800/325-8007, www.enterprise.com), **Hertz** (800/654-3131, www.hertz.com), or **Thrifty** (800/367-2277, www.thrifty.com) in order to reach your hotel or primary destination in Key West.

By Bus or Train

To reach Key West using the regional bus system, you can take the **Miami-Dade County Metrobus** (305/891-3131, www.miamidade.gov/transit), which operates the **301 Dade-Monroe Express** between Florida City and Marathon (5:15am-8:40pm daily). From Marathon, you can then use the **Lower Keys Shuttle,** operated by the **Key West Department of Transportation (KWDoT)** (305/600-1455, www.kwtransit.com, $4 per ride, $25 weekly, $75 monthly), to complete the rest of your journey. The shuttle runs from Marathon to Key West between 5:30am and 11:15pm daily. Other stops include Bahia Honda State Park, Big Pine Key, and several other Lower Keys. Reduced fares may apply for students under 22 years old, senior citizens over 59 years old, military personnel, and disabled individuals.

As for national transportation companies, while **Greyhound** (800/231-2222, www.greyhound.com) offers bus service to the **Key West Greyhound Station** (3535 S. Roosevelt Blvd., 305/296-9072, 7:30am-11am and 3pm-6pm daily) near the Key West International Airport, **Amtrak** (800/872-7245, www.amtrak.com) only provides train service as far south as Miami. Of course, you can always rent a car or hop a shuttle to reach the Florida Keys.

Transport from Airports and Stations

If you arrive in the Fort Lauderdale-Miami area by plane, bus, or train—or Key West by plane or bus—you can either rent a car or hire a shuttle service to reach your destination in the Key West area. Some of these companies include **Keys Shuttle** (305/289-9997 or 888/765-9997, www.keysshuttle.com, $90-100 per shared ride, $400-450 for exclusive service) and

Keys Tropical Transportation (305/852-3595, www.keystropicaltransportation.com, starting at $130 or $165 per ride, depending on the airport of origin), both of which provide service from the Miami and Fort Lauderdale airports. Another option is **TO'n'FRO** (305/393-0955, www.tonfro.com, $300-400 per luxury sedan ride), a personalized van and car service that offers transportation between the Miami and Fort Lauderdale airports and any destination in the Keys.

By Car

To reach Key West from Miami, simply head south on U.S. 1 (Overseas Hwy.), drive through the Upper, Middle, and Lower Keys—roughly 110 miles from the mainland—and continue toward your destination, likely west of Mile Marker 5. If you're headed from the Everglades via I-75 (Everglades Pkwy.), drive south on U.S. 27, veer right onto SR-997 (Krome Ave.), and follow the signs to U.S. 1. From U.S. 41 (Tamiami Trl.) in the Everglades, head south on SR-997 and continue toward U.S. 1. If you arrive during the peak season (Dec.-Apr.), be sure to call **511** for an up-to-the-minute traffic report.

By Boat

As an alternative to planes, buses, and the like, you can also reach Key West by boat. The **Key West Express** (888/539-2628, www.seakeywestexpress.com, $86-147 adults, $20-40 children under 13, $86-135 seniors 62 and over) offers a fleet of comfortable jet-powered passenger ferries that provide year-round daily service from Fort Myers Beach to Key West—a ride that typically takes 3.5 hours. Passengers can opt for one-way travel, same-day return, or different-day return and, with certain restrictions, may be allowed to bring pets and bicycles on board. All passengers 18 years of age and older must present valid identification in order to ride.

GETTING AROUND
By Car

If you're not on foot or a bicycle, the third best

way to travel through Key West is by car or motorcycle—both of which offer easy access to U.S. 1 as well as the residential roads throughout this compact city. The smaller the vehicle, the easier it will be to find street parking when necessary; just remember to watch for parking signs and feed any required meters. Note, too, that Key West offers a few public parking areas in Old Town, including the **Park N' Ride Old Town Garage** (305/809-3910, www.keywestcity.com, $2 hourly, $13 daily) at the corner of Grinnell and Caroline Streets, not far from the Historic Seaport. The garage provides covered overnight parking and convenient access to tourist attractions, and as a bonus, parking here allows you free, same-day access to the city's public transportation.

By Tour or Public Transit

Since Key West is the most populated—and most popular—destination in the Florida Keys, it's not surprising that there are public transit options in addition to taxicabs, pedicabs, and vehicle rentals. Upon arriving in town, you might want to opt for the **Conch Tour Train** (888/916-8687, www.conchtourtrain.com, 9am-4:30pm daily, $30 adults, $27 seniors and military personnel, free for children under 13 and Key West residents) or the **Old Town Trolley Tour** (305/296-6688 or 888/910-8687, www.trolleytours.com, 9am-4:30pm daily, $30 adults, $27 seniors and military personnel, free for children under 13), both of which offer guided excursions through the city—an ideal way to get an overview of all available attractions before exploring them in more depth. In addition, the **Key West Department of Transportation (KWDoT)** (305/600-1455, www.kwtransit.com, $2-3 per ride, $8-16 weekly, $25-50 monthly) provides bus service around Key West and the Lower Keys between 5am and 11pm daily.

By Taxi

Taxicab companies can also help you get around Key West, such as **Perfect Pedicab** (305/292-0077, $1.50 per minute), offering three-wheeled open-air human-operated vehicles, and **Five 6's** (305/296-6666, www.keywesttaxi.com, $2.75 for first 0.2-mile, $0.60 per each additional 0.2-mile), which provides 24-hour service with its pink ecofriendly hybrids that you'll spot seemingly everywhere.

By Bicycle or Boat

Key West is a lovely, welcoming place to traverse by bicycle, whether you're an experienced rider or a novice. Just remember that you'll have to share the streets with cars and other vehicles, so take care while you tour the neighborhoods.

Bicycles can be rented from several different outfitters, including **Eaton Bikes** (830 Eaton St., 305/294-8188, www.eatonbikes.com, 9am-6pm Mon.-Sat., 9am-4pm Sun., $18-45 daily, $40-135 weekly), which offers a range of bicycles, from trikes to mountain bikes to tandems, plus free delivery service throughout Key West. **The Bike Shop of Key West** (1110 Truman Ave., 305/294-1073, www.thebikeshopkeywest.com, 9am-6pm Mon.-Sat., 10am-4pm Sun., $12 daily, $60 weekly, $180 monthly), the oldest in town, also provides a wide array of bicycles, plus accessories, bicycle sales, and a service/repair department. All rentals include locks, lights, baskets, and soft wide seats.

Another helpful source is **Adventure Rentals** (305/293-8883, www.keywest-scooter.com, 9am-5pm daily, $15 daily, $60 weekly), which provides bicycle rentals at multiple locations (0 Duval Street, 617 Front Street, 135 Simonton Street, and Cruise Ship Pier B), plus scooters ($50-70 daily), Harley motorcycles (starting from $268 daily, $935 weekly), and multiple-passenger electric cars ($159-202 daily).

In addition, **A&M Rentals** (305/896-1921, www.amscooterskeywest.com, 8am-8pm daily, $15 daily, $85 weekly) features three spots where you can rent kid-size bicycles, cruisers, and tandems: 523 Truman Avenue, 513 South Street, and 500 Truman Avenue. Here you can also rent one-seater scooters ($35 daily, $109 weekly), two-seater scooters ($55 daily, $179 weekly), and multi-seater electric cars ($99 daily)—all popular ways to get around town. Free customer pickup and drop-off services are available. Take note that such outfitters typically require that all electric car operators possess a valid driver's license and be at least 21 or 22 years old.

You can also experience Key West by boat. Having your own vessel makes navigating these waters even easier, and you'll find no shortage of marinas in the area. If you'd rather rent a boat, stop by **Sunset Watersports Key West** (Hurricane Hole Marina, 5130 Overseas Hwy., Stock Island, 305/294-5500, www.sunsetwatersports.info), which offers a range of vessels, from 17-foot fishing boats ($250 per half day, $325 daily) to 24-foot pontoons ($400 per half day, $500 daily). Also at the Hurricane Hole Marina, you'll find **Lazy Dog** (305/295-9898, www.lazydog.com), which offers two-hour guided kayak tours ($35 pp) in addition to kayak rentals ($20 per half day, $30 daily).

Dry Tortugas National Park

Roughly 68 miles west of Key West lies a cluster of seven islands, composed of coral and sand that are collectively known as the Dry Tortugas. Originally named Las Tortugas (The Turtles) by Spanish explorers, the islands eventually became "Dry Tortugas" on mariners' navigational charts to indicate the lack of fresh water here. Part of the 220-mile-long Florida Keys archipelago, these islands, in addition to the surrounding shoals and waters, comprise the 64,657-acre **Dry Tortugas National Park,** established in 1992 to preserve this unique area and now one of the most remote parks in the National Park System. In addition, Dry Tortugas has been listed on the National Register of Historic Places.

Celebrated for its diverse wildlife, its remarkable coral reefs, its enthralling shipwrecks, and its pirate legends and military past, Dry Tortugas is indeed a must-see destination, the kind of place that really makes you feel as though you're a world away from the Florida mainland. If you have the time, you should definitely board a ferry or come by private boat to this unique destination—popular with sunbathers, swimmers, snorkelers, kayakers, anglers, bird-watchers, photographers, and overnight campers.

SIGHTS
While visiting the Dry Tortugas, you should take a guided or self-guided tour of **Fort Jefferson,** the well-preserved Civil War fort on Garden Key, the centerpiece of these remote islands. Nicknamed the "American Gibraltar," the country's largest 19th-century, coastal fort was initially established in 1846 in order to control navigation in the Gulf of Mexico, though its construction was never quite completed. During and after the war, it served as a remote, Union-affiliated military prison for

Fort Jefferson, part of Dry Tortugas National Park

© ANDY NEWMAN/FLORIDA KEYS NEWS BUREAU

captured deserters. From 1865 to 1869 it was even home to Dr. Samuel Mudd, who was incarcerated here for setting the broken leg of assassin John Wilkes Booth and thereby participating in the assassination of President Abraham Lincoln. By the 1880s the U.S. Army had abandoned the facility, which became a wildlife refuge in 1908 and a national monument in 1935. An interesting tidbit is that in 1847 seven enslaved African Americans fled Garden Key in a dramatic self-emancipation attempt. Although they were ultimately caught, their daring effort has been officially acknowledged by the National Underground Railroad Network to Freedom Program.

Within the fortified walls of this historical citadel, you'll encounter such sites as the officers' quarters, soldiers' barracks, cistern, magazines, and cannons. The visitor center and park headquarters are also located here. From November to May, parts of Fort Jefferson are closed to the public while mason crews work on much-needed preservation projects. Such temporary closures are not in effect during the hurricane season (June-Nov.), which might only add to the logistical difficulties of this remote marine environment. Note that pets, food, and drinks are not allowed inside the fort. In addition, service and residential areas are closed to the public.

While visiting Fort Jefferson, be sure to take a look at the **Fort Jefferson Harbor Light,** northeast of the boat dock. Established in 1825 and still operational today, the lighthouse, whose present tower was erected in 1876, is a favorite among photographers. In addition, Loggerhead Key, which once housed the Carnegie Institute's Laboratory of Marine Ecology and is only accessible by private boat or charter, features the **Loggerhead Light,** also established in 1825, with an existing tower that was erected in 1858. Just remember that all buildings and structures on Loggerhead Key are closed to visitors, unless accompanied by a park ranger.

RECREATION

Although visiting Dry Tortugas National Park is only possible by ferry or private boat, the isolated **Fort Jefferson Beach** is well worth the trip. Besides its proximity to historical Fort Jefferson, it's a terrific locale for swimming, snorkeling, kayaking, fishing, and bird-watching. Certain activities are prohibited, such as spearfishing, lobstering, using personal watercraft, collecting artifacts and marinelife, bartering with commercial fishermen for seafood, or possessing loaded firearms in federal facilities.

Bird-Watching and Wildlife-Viewing

Many people come to Garden Key for the bird-watching opportunities, which are truly excellent out here. More than 200 varieties are spotted annually, especially from March through September, when nearby Bush Key serves as the nesting grounds for migratory birds. During April and May, over 85,000 brown noddies and sooty terns nest on Bush Key. In the spring you might spot herons, raptors, and shorebirds, and in summertime you might observe frigatebirds and mourning doves. The fall and winter months bring such species as hawks, merlins, peregrine falcons, gulls, terns, American kestrels, and belted kingfishers. Other possible sightings include orioles, warbles, cormorants, masked boobies, black noddies, mangrove cuckoos, and white-crowned pigeons. Be sure to pick up an official bird checklist from the visitor center in Fort Jefferson, or consult the **Audubon Society of Florida** (Keys Environmental Restoration Trust, 11399 Overseas Hwy., Ste. 4E, Marathon, 305/289-9988, http://fl.audubon. org) for more information.

While you can spot many of these species during a short visit to Garden or Loggerhead Keys, you might have a better experience on board a bird-watching charter—though admittedly a pricier one as well. **Sea-Clusive Charters** (1107 Key Plaza, Ste. 315, Key West, 305/744-9928, www.seaclusive.com, $2,600-3,275 per trip) features such tailored excursions, led by professional bird guide Larry Manfredi (www.southfloridabirding.com). While on board, you might also spot other wildlife, such as sharks, dolphins, and if you're lucky, gigantic sea turtles. These cruises can accommodate a minimum of eight passengers and a maximum of 11.

Boating and Kayaking

Since Garden Key and Loggerhead Key are both accessible by private boat, many boaters enjoy this park as well. Unfortunately, the dock on Loggerhead Key is only open to government vessels, but luckily, you're allowed to land south of the boathouse. Docking on Garden Key can also be problematic, as the public dock is often occupied by ferries and supply boats. Given that you can only tie up to the dock for two-hour increments between sunrise and 10am and then again between 3pm and sunset, your best bet is to anchor in the harbor and use a dinghy to reach the island, which offers a dinghy beach for that exact purpose. Overnight anchoring, between sunset and sunrise, is only allowed in the designated anchorage area: the sand and rubble bottom within one nautical mile of the Fort Jefferson Harbor Light.

All boaters should have self-sufficient, fully equipped vessels. Necessary items include life jackets, nautical charts, a tool kit with spare parts, plenty of fuel and drinking water, and a VHF radio to monitor weather forecasts. In addition, all vessels must conform to U.S. Coast Guard regulations.

Kayaking can also be a wonderful way to experience the islands, though you'll need to take care. The currents here can be very strong, making the area suitable for experienced sea kayakers only. If you do choose to tote kayaks along for the ride, make sure to bring a life vest, an anchor, a bailer, extra paddles, drinking water, and waterproof bags for gear. Other necessary safety equipment includes flares, bow and stern lines, a sound-producing device, a 360-degree light for operating at night, and the NOAA nautical chart #11438.

Fishing

Anglers are welcome to fish from the public dock on Garden Key, as well as the beach west of the dock. With the recent establishment of the 46-square-mile Research Natural Area (RNA), however, fishing from a boat is only permitted within a one-mile radius of Garden Key. Nevertheless, several local fishing charters operate multiday trips to this area. With proper permits and licenses, these guides are allowed to fish in and around Dry Tortugas National Park. **Andy Griffiths Charters** (40 Key Haven Rd., Key West, 305/296-2639, www.fishandy. com), for instance, offers three-day, two-night excursions ($3,000-3,600) to the Dry Tortugas for up to six anglers. These trips typically last from 10am on Friday to 2pm on Sunday, or from noon on Monday to 2pm on Wednesday.

Dream Catcher Charters (5555 College Rd., Stock Island, 305/292-7702 or 888/362-3474, www.chartersofkeywest.com), meanwhile, offers 10-hour trips ($900-950) for up to six passengers as well as overnight excursions (trip times and rates vary). Another helpful operator is **Lethal Weapon Charters** (1418 Angela St., Key West, 305/296-6999 or 305/744-8225, www.lethalweaponcharters.com, trip times and rates vary). Of course, if you choose instead to fish on your own, remember that Florida state laws, regulations, and licensing requirements apply in these waters. Commercial fishing, spearfishing, taking fish by sling or speargun, dragging a net, casting near sea turtles, collecting shells and artifacts, and possessing lobster, conch, or ornamental tropical fish are not allowed within the boundaries of Dry Tortugas National Park.

Diving and Snorkeling

With numerous patch reefs and shipwrecks, including the 19th-century Bird Key Wreck and early 20th-century Windjammer Wreck, within the boundaries of Dry Tortugas National Park, it's no wonder that snorkelers, scuba divers, and underwater photographers favor this area. Whether you arrive on Garden Key by ferry or private boat, you'll be able to snorkel directly off the beach, near the moat walls and coaling dock ruins, in warm, shallow waters that boast a cornucopia of kaleidoscopic tropical fish, conch shells, lobster and sponges, sea fans and sea anemones, staghorn coral clusters, and occasional sea turtles.

For access to even more snorkeling and scuba-diving sites around the Dry Tortugas—part of Florida Keys National Marine Sanctuary—consult **Sea-Clusive Charters** (1107 Key Plaza, Ste. 315, Key West, 305/744-9928, www.seaclusive.com, $2,600-3,275 per trip), which offers multiday diving excursions for 6-11 passengers. With Sea-Clusive, divers will be able to explore the Windjammer wreck site as well as the overhangs, caves, and swim troughs of these incredible coral reefs, which offer water depths of 45 to 80 feet. Here you'll spot tropical fish, resident jewfish, black grouper, coral formations, and sponges.

If you choose to snorkel or dive on your own, you should be aware of certain offshore protection zones that are closed to the public. In addition, you need to prepare for potentially strong gulf currents. Remember, too, that dive flags are required beyond designated swimming channels at all times.

CAMPING

Since Dry Tortugas National Park has no public lodging, camping is the only option for those who hope to stay overnight on Garden Key. Just a short southwesterly walk from the public dock lies a primitive 10-site campground. Although the group site, which must be reserved in advance, can accommodate 10-40 people, most of the sites are available on a first-come, first-served basis and will suit up to six people and three tents. The campground is a self-service fee area, charging a nightly fee of $3 per person, and the sites offer little more than picnic tables and barbecue grills.

Grocery stores, fresh water, ice, and fuel are unavailable here, so plan accordingly. No trash receptacles are present either, which means that all visitors, boaters, and campers must pack out any and all trash. Unless you plan to anchor a private boat in the harbor near Garden Key, you'll probably be reaching the park by a commercial ferry. If so, be aware that most transportation companies have cargo weight restrictions. On the *Yankee Freedom II*, for instance, campers are limited to 60 pounds of gear plus water, while campers arriving aboard the Sunny Days

Fast Cat are limited to 40 pounds of gear plus water. Neither ferry allows the transport of fuels like propane or lighter fluid, so campers are encouraged to use self-starting charcoal.

In order to make your camping trip as smooth as possible, there are several items you should be sure to pack, including picture identification, a fishing license, camping regulations, and the current weather forecast. To make your stay more comfortable, bring along a tent, a sleeping bag and pad, rain gear, clothing for warm and cold weather, a wide-brimmed hat, and plenty of food, water, and ice. Cooking equipment should include a portable stove or grill, fuel of some kind, waterproof matches and a lighter, cooking utensils, biodegradable soap, and trash bags. Personal gear, such as medications, a first-aid kit, a knife, a flashlight and spare batteries, sunglasses, sunscreen, and insect repellent, will also prove to be helpful. Although you can bring pets with you, they are only allowed on Garden Key, outside Fort Jefferson, and must be leashed and well-behaved at all times. It probably goes without saying that owners must remove all pet waste from the park. Campers are only allowed to stay for four days and three nights at a time.

INFORMATION

Technically, Dry Tortugas National Park is open all year, though restrictions are in effect on certain islands. Garden Key, which contains Fort Jefferson, is surely the most visited island in the park. Although the island itself is open year-round, Fort Jefferson is only open during daylight hours. Loggerhead is also open year-round during daylight hours. Middle and East Keys, however, are closed from April to mid-October during turtle nesting season, while Bush, Hospital, and Long Keys are closed all year, meaning that visitors should remain 100 feet offshore of these particular islands.

To visit the park, anyone 16 years of age or older must pay an entrance fee of $5. The pass, which is valid for seven days, is typically collected by commercial transportation operators; otherwise, you'll have to remit payment at the Garden Key visitor center. Annual passes, which can be purchased or procured at the **Florida Keys Eco-Discovery Center (FKEDC)** (35 E. Quay Rd., Key West, 305/809-4750, www.floridakeys.noaa.gov, 9am-4pm Tues.-Sat., free) with qualifying documentation, are all honored in Dry Tortugas. These include the National Parks and Federal Recreational Lands Pass ($80) and the lifetime versions for senior citizens 62 years of age and older ($10), disabled visitors (free), and volunteers (free)—plus the now-discontinued Golden Eagle, Golden Age, and Golden Access Passports. All such passes are only eligible to legal U.S. citizens and permanent residents.

The recently designated, 46-square-mile Research Natural Area (RNA)—an ecological preserve that will encompass a little less than half of the park and serves to protect species affected by overfishing and loss of habitat—may eventually limit your fishing access to certain areas and require permits in other areas. For more information about Dry Tortugas National Park, including details about the RNA, contact the **park headquarters** (305/242-7700, www.nps.gov/drto/index.htm, 8am-4:30pm Mon.-Fri.) or the Florida Keys Eco-Discovery Center. You can also consult websites like www.dry.tortugas.national-park.com. In addition, you can download park maps and regulations, plus information about camping, bird-watching, island history, and the RNA, from the official National Park Service website. Books are also helpful resources, such as Thomas Reid's *America's Fortress: A History of Fort Jefferson, Dry Tortugas, Florida* (Gainesville, FL: University Press of Florida, 2006).

GETTING THERE AND AROUND

Dry Tortugas National Park, which lies approximately 68 miles west of Key West, is only accessible by ferry or private boat—all of which can be boarded in Key West. (Incidentally, seaplanes used to be a viable way to reach Garden Key, but the company has indefinitely suspended such trips, pending legal action.) To reach Garden Key by ferry, you can schedule a day trip on the 100-foot catamaran **Yankee**

Freedom II (240 Margaret St., 305/294-7009 or 800/322-0013, www.yankeefreedom.com, 8am-5:30pm daily, $165 adults, $155 students, military personnel, and seniors 62 and over, $120 children 4-16, free for children under 4), which is docked in the Historic Seaport at Key West Bight. Reservations are recommended for the ferry, which will charge an additional park entrance fee of $5 per person aged 16 or over. Cancellations must be made the day before your scheduled trip, and all passengers should arrive no later than 7:30am on the day of departure. In addition to day trips, the ferry offers overnight excursions, for which reservations are absolutely required. The *Yankee Freedom II* charges $180 for adult campers and $140 for children; however, such rates do not include the requisite park entrance and camping fees.

For the ferry, which has comfortable air-conditioned cabins, the day trip from Key West begins at 8am. While you journey past the Marquesas, the famous *Atocha* shipwreck, and various marinelife, you'll be treated to a complimentary continental breakfast. Once you arrive on Garden Key, you can opt for a 45-minute narrated tour of Fort Jefferson with one of the ferries' knowledgeable guides, after which you can relax on the pristine beach, go for a swim, have a picnic, or take a bird-watching nature stroll. In addition, you'll have free use of the on-board snorkeling equipment. It's recommended that you bring a swimsuit and towel, sun protection, a camera and batteries, binoculars, sunglasses, water shoes, a jacket, and a hat. A reliable watch is also necessary, as the ferry will leave around 3pm in order to reach Key West by late afternoon.

If you choose to travel to Garden Key by private vessel, bear in mind the docking restrictions, which limit your use of the public dock between the hours of sunrise and 10am, and between 3pm and sunset. On Loggerhead Key, which is only accessible by private boat or charter, you can only land your vessel south of the dock and boathouse. Once on the island, you can explore the developed trails and shoreline, but remember that the dock and all structures are closed to the public.

www.moon.com

DESTINATIONS | ACTIVITIES | BLOGS | MAPS | BOOKS

MOON.COM is ready to help plan your next trip! Filled with fresh trip ideas and strategies, author interviews, informative travel blogs, a detailed map library, and descriptions of all the Moon guidebooks, Moon.com is all you need to get out and explore the world—or even places in your own backyard. While at Moon.com, sign up for our monthly e-newsletter for updates on new releases, travel tips, and expert advice from our on-the-go Moon authors. As always, when you travel with Moon, expect an experience that is uncommon and truly unique.

KEEP UP WITH MOON ON FACEBOOK AND TWITTER JOIN THE MOON PHOTO GROUP ON FLICKR

MAP SYMBOLS

▭▭▭ Expressway	◖ Highlight	✗ Airfield	⚑ Golf Course
⋯⋯ Primary Road	○ City/Town	✈ Airport	⊡ Parking Area
▬▬ Secondary Road	◉ State Capital	▲ Mountain	▲ Archaeological Site
⋯⋯ Unpaved Road	⊛ National Capital	✚ Unique Natural Feature	⛪ Church
------ Trail	★ Point of Interest		☗ Gas Station
⋯⋯ Ferry	• Accommodation	⚐ Waterfall	〰 Glacier
⊶⊶ Railroad	▼ Restaurant/Bar	▲ Park	⬚ Mangrove
▭▭ Pedestrian Walkway	▪ Other Location	⬛ Trailhead	▨ Reef
⊞⊞ Stairs	∧ Campground	⚐ Skiing Area	⬚ Swamp

CONVERSION TABLES

$°C = (°F - 32) / 1.8$
$°F = (°C \times 1.8) + 32$
1 inch = 2.54 centimeters (cm)
1 foot = 0.304 meters (m)
1 yard = 0.914 meters
1 mile = 1.6093 kilometers (km)
1 km = 0.6214 miles
1 fathom = 1.8288 m
1 chain = 20.1168 m
1 furlong = 201.168 m
1 acre = 0.4047 hectares
1 sq km = 100 hectares
1 sq mile = 2.59 square km
1 ounce = 28.35 grams
1 pound = 0.4536 kilograms
1 short ton = 0.90718 metric ton
1 short ton = 2,000 pounds
1 long ton = 1.016 metric tons
1 long ton = 2,240 pounds
1 metric ton = 1,000 kilograms
1 quart = 0.94635 liters
1 US gallon = 3.7854 liters
1 Imperial gallon = 4.5459 liters
1 nautical mile = 1.852 km

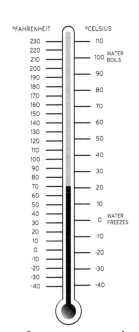

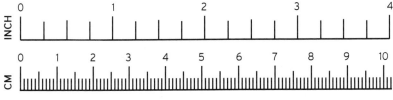

MOON SPOTLIGHT KEY WEST
Avalon Travel
a member of the Perseus Books Group
1700 Fourth Street
Berkeley, CA 94710, USA
www.moon.com

Editor: Leah Gordon
Series Manager: Kathryn Ettinger
Copy Editor: Carolyn Cotney
Graphics Coordinator: Darren Alessi
Production Coordinator: Darren Alessi
Cover Designer: Kathryn Osgood
Map Editor: Albert Angulo
Cartographers: Albert Angulo, Kat Bennett,
  Stephanie Poulain, Brian Shotwell

ISBN-13: 978-1-61238-886-1

Text © 2013 by Laura Martone.
Maps © 2013 by Avalon Travel.
All rights reserved.

Front cover photo: Key West Florida, Bridge & Palm
  Tree # 858984 © Mark Van Lue | Dreamstime.com
Title page photo: © Andy Newman/Florida Keys News
  Bureau/HO

Printed in the United States

All recommendations, including those for sights,
  activities, hotels, restaurants, and shops, are based
  on each author's individual judgment. We do not
  accept payment for inclusion in our travel guides,
  and our authors don't accept free goods or services
  in exchange for positive coverage.

Although every effort was made to ensure that the
  information was correct at the time of going to
  press, the author and publisher do not assume and
  hereby disclaim any liability to any party for any
  loss or damage caused by errors, omissions, or any
  potential travel disruption due to labor or financial
  difficulty, whether such errors or omissions result
  from negligence, accident, or any other cause.

ABOUT THE AUTHOR

Laura Martone

Fond of both cultural and natural wonders, Laura Martone particularly adores the Florida Keys, which she's been exploring for decades. She's snorkeled amid the coral reefs east of Key Largo, watched dragon boat races near Marathon, savored key lime pie on Duval Street, and visited the former haunts of Ernest Hemingway. While she favors outdoorsy places like Bahia Honda State Park, she feels a definite kinship for Key West, a town that's at once lively and laid-back, where she's spent many perfect afternoons strolling amid the gingerbread-like Victorian houses and breezy, Caribbean-style bungalows.

A native of New Orleans, Laura has been an avid traveler since childhood. While growing up, she and her mother would often take long road trips to fascinating U.S. landmarks, from Monticello to the Rocky Mountains. After graduating from Northwestern University with a dual degree in English and radio/TV/film, Laura continued to explore America with her husband, Daniel.

When not traveling, Laura operates two film festivals with her husband and divides her time between New Orleans, Los Angeles, and northern Michigan. She's contributed articles to *National Geographic Traveler, MotorHome, Route 66 Magazine, RV Journal,* and *The Ecotourism Observer,* and she's also written several other guidebooks, including *Moon New Orleans, Moon Michigan, and Moon Baja RV Camping.* For more about Laura's travels, visit her website at www.wanderingsoles.com.